SOUL VISION

SOUL VISION

A modern mystic looks at life
through the eyes of the soul

BILL BAUMAN, PH.D.

THE CENTER FOR SOULFUL LIVING

A CENTER FOR SOULFUL LIVING PUBLICATION

The Center for Soulful Living
P.O. Box 583
St. George, UT 84771-0583
USA
www.aboutcsl.com

FIRST EDITION, 2009

Cover design by Donna Bauman
Book design by Jo Anne Smith

ISBN 978-0-692-00004-5

PRINTED IN THE UNITED STATES OF AMERICA

To

Donna

Surreal partner

Gracious lover of life

Gorgeous loving woman

Expression of the angelic heart

Quiet essence gracefully expressed

Embodiment of the feminine spirit

Beauty elegantly placed in human body

Woman I am honored to call lover

Woman I am honored to love

Blessing and gift to life

Pure gift to me

Thank you

Bill

ACKNOWLEDGMENTS

What a privilege it is to write a book that is truly the collective voice of the thousands of people who have influenced, taught and inspired me throughout my life! I sincerely believe that I am among the world's most blessed human beings, mainly because life has lovingly placed me under the influence of so many remarkable, amazing and beautiful persons. If you know me or have even met me briefly, you're one of those—and I thank you for the ways in which you have so generously, if unknowingly, given me the benefit of the sacred gift called you.

In the lengthy preparation of this book, I am especially indebted to two gifted literary giants, both of whom also happen to be equally exceptional persons. The first of these is my dear friend Cynthia Lane, who so generously lent her incomparable writing skills, gift of expansive thinking, and pure, devoted heart to the initial draft of the book's beginning chapters. Cynthia, I thank you for the mystical presence, skilled writer and dynamic spirit that you are, in my life and in that of so many others.

The second of these blessing-filled helpers is Jo Anne Smith, the book's official editor and designer, as well as a cherished personal friend. Jo Anne, you have my unending gratitude both for your indescribably delicious editorial gifts, and for the priceless ways in which you tailor those gifts so masterfully to my unique spirit and message. This book is truly blessed not only by your notable literary talent, intuitive sense and inspired touch, but equally by your mystical nature and empowering soul.

I also owe a cherished debt of gratitude to Charlie Werner, an accomplished attorney and my good friend, for his selfless and generous help in the complex task of securing permission to use the many quotations that you will find throughout this book.

Beyond these above influences, however, I thank you, the reader. Yes, you. Whether you have known me or never heard of me, your very soulfulness and our rich oneness have contributed deeply to the pure spirit and heartful touch of this book.

Finally, and especially, I am privileged to express my deepest appreciation and love to Donna Bauman, my beautiful and cherished life partner. Appreciation, Donna, for the countless, selfless hours that you gave to skillfully reading and honestly critiquing the many drafts of this book. Love, for being the most wondrous, loving and dazzling partner any human being could ever wish for. I am daily blessed by the majesty of your penetrating presence, the beauty of your quiet femininity and the power of your angelic spirit. In short, Donna, thank you for being such an ever-present, stunning gift in my life. I love you.

CONTENTS

INTRODUCTION

Welcome to a unique vision of life! I've written this book to give you an uplifting and inspiring perspective on the nature of life and our shared human experience—its singular origins, its mysterious dynamics, its inspired purposes and its magical, creative possibilities.

This unique worldview came to me over several years as I sat on my personal perch over the forest of life, soulfully contemplating humanity's oldest and most persistent questions: What is the nature and meaning of life? What's it all about?

I'm offering you this vision and inviting you to become an intimate partner to its possibilities for one reason—so you can apply it to your life and live here on earth with more freedom, peace, delight and grace. My wish and intention is that, through this special insight into our shared life, you will find the hidden fruits of life's bounty and nourish yourself with them every day.

Many beliefs about life—philosophical, religious, political, cultural, spiritual and more—have come and gone through the centuries. Each one has served an important purpose for a given period of time and played a helpful role for a particular group of people. Eventually, each has been reshaped or replaced by newer modes of thinking. With this rhythmic, ongoing cycle of ever-expanding ideas, our human family has grown its awareness, become increasingly creative and taken greater charge of its destiny. In short, each perspective has been just right for its time and circumstances.

Now, I am offering a fresh look at our shared experience. In doing so, I'm in no way implying any judgment about other approaches to human living or happiness. They're all fine, just as they are. In fact, I genuinely honor the multiple and varied paradigms that surround us—in fact, we need all of them. Each of us is so distinctive that no one system of belief or behavior can speak meaningfully to all of us. In truth, our existing philosophies and theologies deserve our sincere respect.

Why, then, do we need yet another picture of our lives and ourselves? For two reasons. First, because we're still struggling. Despite abundant sources of knowledge, wisdom and inspiration, world peace is not yet in

The real voyage of discovery consists not in seeking new lands but in seeing with new eyes.

MARCEL PROUST [1]

sight, conflict still plagues so much of our human family, and personal happiness continues to elude many of us. Clearly, we've not yet learned to use our prevailing wisdom effectively.

More important though, our human family is all about growing and expanding. It's in our created nature to evolve, so that we can become more and more of our enormous potential. With each age of expanding possibility, such as today's, a fresh and fuller vision is needed. With it as our inspirational guide, we can spring headlong into our destiny.

Thus, this book responds to a genuine human need—the need for a worldview that is more freeing for us, individually and collectively. I offer this vision because we truly have come to a moment of possibility here on earth. Our human family has made dramatic strides in science, technology and consciousness over the recent past, and these changes have prepared us, deep in our psyches, to embrace a larger panorama of life's nature and meanings. We're ready to leap.

So, here it is: an expanded picture of life's potentials, a bigger grasp of its profound nature, a more meaningful connection to the compelling purposes of human living … and, hopefully, a way to more fully experience the innate wonder and power of this mysterious existence of which we are a part.

A MYSTIC'S VIEW

I'm a mystic. There, I said it, the very three-word sentence that few of us would dare to utter. Deep in your heart, you know that you're a mystic too. We're all mystics. Every one of us has an undeniably mystical side—an aspect of ourselves that lives above the forest of life, experiences insights from a larger realm, and yearns for the same inner peace known intimately by the world's acknowledged mystics.

In fact, you wouldn't be reading this page unless something deeply mystical within you prompted you to pick this book up. So, let's agree— it's okay to claim your mystical nature. In that spirit, I ask you to join with me in this soulful exploration of life.

Being mystical, I have discovered, is both wondrous and challenging. Its wondrous quality is obvious: I am privileged to live life in its pure simplicity and awe-inspiring mystery. The feeling of personal oneness with all life, intimate participation with the divine's creative magic, and deep grounding in true inner peace is, as they say, "out of this world"—except that, for me, it's ever so much a real part of this world's experience.

What we humans are looking for in a creation story is a way of experiencing the world that will open us to the transcendent, that informs us and at the same time forms ourselves within it. That is what people want. That is what the soul asks for.

JOSEPH CAMPBELL[2]

The challenging aspect of being a mystic is also easy to guess. Simply, there aren't many people to talk to about it. Since our shared mystical quality is not a common topic of conversation, most of us are too embarrassed to mention our latest above-the-forest inkling or mystery-filled experience.

That's where you come in. I'm writing this book for you, so that you can use its concepts as a springboard to claim your own mystical awareness more fully and to make your life richer and more dynamic. For that purpose, I invite you to listen trustingly to your own intuitive thoughts and soulful promptings as you take in my written words.

THE SOUL'S VISION

A simple definition of a mystic is someone who lives full time in the loving embrace, empowering gifts and pure vision of the soul. As we know, the word *soul* refuses to be tied down to a specific definition—it chooses rather to remain intangible, ethereal and ungraspable. In this more subtle and mystery-clad mode, the soul is free to inspire, thrill and stir us endlessly.

Our very own soul is a phenomenal source of wisdom, which we can easily fail to notice as it lies so quietly and permissively within our depths. Yet this amazing inner guide offers us a remarkably expansive view of life when we dare to look through its all-seeing eyes.

That's what this book offers you: a mystical view of life—terrestrial and far beyond—as seen through the soul's unique perspective. As I've sat with, in and as this ever-present soul—listening to its wisdom, uncovering its truth, and being awed by its all-knowingness—I've discovered the following vision of life:

- *Essence* (Chapter 1): All there is, at its core, is unlimited Being, the is-ness of life that we have come to call the divine. This totally self-contained essence *is*—that's all that can be said about it. Each of us shares in this pure essence; we find it in the quiet intimacy of our soul.

- *Light* (Chapter 2): The creative dream of life begins: Let there be light! Essence exploded itself brightly in luminescence, thus creating a brilliant mirror of its unspeakable grandeur. In turn, light gave birth to endless stars, ever-inventive photons and an endless field of spectacular radiance. Each of us lives intimately in this glowing light field—indeed, we are beings of light—and can directly experience light's renewing, enlivening radiance.

- *Energy* (Chapter 3): Light subsequently birthed itself into an energy-rich creative field, propelled by the unique energetic force that we have come to call love. Thus was born the distinctive energy vortex called earth and the dynamic miracle called the human family. Each of us is fed and moved daily by energy's unlimited gifts, never-ending powers and creative possibilities.

- *Conscious Awareness* (Chapter 4): We humans inherited a unique gift—we can become fully aware of ourselves, others and life. Through this distinctive endowment of consciousness, we can not only navigate our way through the compelling challenges of our human existence, but we can actually become the radiant light beings that we naturally are and live peacefully in the pure essence of life.

- *Living the Vision* (Chapter 5): Once we have felt the calling of this vision and said yes to its inspiring invitations, we're free to use its possibilities for endless growth and expansion. We can now live in *essence's* innermost harbor of being and peace, travel comfortably in *light's* multidimensional realms, take charge of our *energies* like never before, and merge our human *consciousness* with that of the infinite. In short, we can now live the dream's intended purpose and complete its, and our, creative design.

Life, to me, is not only mysterious, it's positively exciting. The utter perfection of every moment, the intrinsic beauty of each person, and the dynamic radiance of life itself are right here within our grasp. I truly believe that many, many of us today—and that includes you—are ready to awaken to this pure experience of life.

We humans have spent so much time trying to achieve happiness and inner peace through changing things—ourselves, others, perceived problems, etc. Somehow, we have adopted the belief that, if we can but change what we see, our pain will go away, we will be happier, and we can finally enjoy life's perfection—after the serious effort is done.

It simply doesn't work that way. As Marcel Proust wrote, "The real voyage of discovery consists not in seeking new lands but in seeing with new eyes." That's my purpose: to help us see with new eyes, the refreshing eyes of the soul. With this grand inner and cosmic perception, our vision pierces through our limiting viewpoints and opens to life's exciting possibilities. We look beyond the smaller definitions of self to an inner beauty that truly can set us free. We re-discover life's wonder, revel in its mystery, and find delight in its creations. We need change nothing; we need simply to see and embrace the truth.

The simplest, purest truth is this: we all can make a profound connection with life's infinite riches, welcome its many gifts into our experience, and watch those gifts transform our lives. Then, we can merge our identity with life itelf, become it in our innermost experience, and know ourselves as the vast beings that we are born to be.

In short, each of us can make a mystical leap into the magnificence of life's bounty, without leaving the sweet home of our innermost being.

May this adventure in reading lead you into the magical and miraculous wonder of life! May you rediscover the grandeur of your own divine nature, find liberating wings of radiant light, and enjoy this energy-rich world of human possibilities like never before!

NOTES OF SENSITIVITY

I frequently refer to the divine throughout this book. We all know that God cannot be defined by or limited to concepts of gender. Yet, when using pronouns and adjectives, I had to arbitrarily choose words that personalize our creative source, while also showing respect for our many styles of perceiving God.

I've chosen not to refer to our divine source as "He," as is our historical practice. Such a reference can seem gender-biased and limiting. It also seems clumsy to alternate references to God as "he," "she" or "it," chapter-by-chapter, as some writers do.

In place of these options, I've chosen to refer to God pronominally as "it." This solution both bypasses the tricky gender issue and invites our focus on God as source, force and presence more than as a seemingly humanized version of itself.

Like you, I understand that there is no accepted, convenient or pleasing way to resolve this issue. Therefore, I hope that you will have compassion for my predicament and tolerate my less than ideal solution.

In addition, I have decided to honor and support the intimacy and naturalness of our bond with God by not capitalizing words that refer to God. For example, Divine is written as "divine," Creator as "creator," Source as "source," and so on. This small change is my subtle but genuine effort to reduce our historical feeling of separation from God.

In doing away with the formality of upper-case letters, I hope that you will feel a little bit closer to this wondrous source that lives so intimately in our hearts and souls.

The one notable exception to this convention, of course, is the word *God*. In this very special case, I have preserved its initial capital letter—to honor the respect that we have all come to associate with that unique divine reference. Some traditions are simply too sacred to change—and capitalizing the name of God is indeed one of them.

Finally, you'll note that I've included many quotations throughout these pages from philosophers, scientists, sages, scriptures and other sources. I've chosen to include their wisdom as an adjunct to my own so you can experience the soul's inspiration and vision from as many angles as possible. If you find them distracting, however, please feel free to ignore them.

God revealed
a sublime truth
to the world
when He sang,
'I am made whole
by your life.
Each soul, each soul
completes me.'

HAFIZ[3]

PROLOGUE:
THE SOUL AS VISIONARY

Soul. This mystery-clad word has slowly become a natural part of our modern language. It connotes, I believe, a compelling, appealing, yet almost indefinable presence that most of us acknowledge as very real. We know that we "have" a soul and that it lives somewhere in the core of us, whether or not we are aware of its powerful presence and loving inspiration.

Over the years, I must admit, this awesome phenomenon called soul has claimed me. It lives solidly in my heart and calls me to dwell in its loving embrace full time, so that I can experience life through its wondrous and magical perspectives. As a result, I've come to know the soul of humanity intimately and to experience each human being in his or her soulful elegance. Filled with the soul's vast vision, I relate to every world event, positive or negative, through the portal of its purest invitations; and I find the soul-inspired truth of any life circumstance, however it may appear on the surface.

So, soul is, to me, a personally rich and centrally compelling marvel of life. It's where the underlying truth of each and every one of us lovingly lives, and it provides that all-seeing perspective that brilliantly captures the hidden secrets of life's intriguing mysteries.

Early on in my personal experience of soul, I discovered that I could no longer think of it only in its singular, individualized sense. I realized that, in the big picture, there is but *one* soul—the unbounded, unified soul of life itself—and we all share its unending gifts. Just as each droplet of sea water contains and expresses the life force of the entire ocean, so each of us is a unique expression of the pure soul of life's vast ocean of possibilities.

There's a common saying that "Life lives us as much as we live life." Well, I found that it's the same with soul: the very soul of life itself lives

Spirit is the life,
mind is the builder,
and the physical is the result.
Realize that you are first a soul.
EDGAR CAYCE[1]

Out beyond ideas of wrongdoing
and right doing there is a field.
I'll meet you there.
When the soul lies down in that
grass
the world is too full to talk about.
RUMI[2]

Once you do a trial run
of living your life
based on a belief in oneness
instead of a belief in separateness,
nothing will ever be the same.
VICTORIA MORAN[3]

As is the microcosm, so is the macrocosm. As is the atom, so is the universe. As is the human body, so is the cosmic body. As is the human mind, so is the cosmic mind.

HINDU SCRIPTURE[4]

A divine ray, atom, soul, call it what you wish, is present in each of us.

PAUL BRUNTON[5]

us. It breathes us, moves in us, and expresses through each of us, every moment of our lives.

Yes, you and I are individualized manifestations of the mighty, magnificent, pure and radiant soul of life. Of course, we can rightly call it our personal soul—but, even so, our soulful experience is intricately linked to that of every other sentient being. Indeed, our individual soul is connected to the very breath and source of life that constitutes the make-up of everyone and everything, everywhere.

So, in this sense, soul is simply our eloquent and inspiring word for the source of life itself—the force that we have come to call divine and that inexplicably infuses its life force into each of us. The infinite is everywhere we look, including right in the middle of our daily finite world and in the precious center of ourselves.

WHAT IS THE SOUL?

I recently felt moved to put words to this awesome gift that is both omnipresent and at the core of each of us. So, I asked the soul of life to speak its identity into my inner ear so that it could make itself somewhat more tangible and substantial—perhaps just for you in this moment. Then, I quietly sat with this mystery-filled, impressive presence called soul, opening myself to its response to these vexing questions: Who are you? What are you? The following is what I heard:

The soul is ...

- the infinite presence, radiating its splendor ... within us

- the divine quality of our own nature ... our God-Self

- the intimate echo of life's pure truth, love and power

The soul is our ...

- inner voice ... innate truth ... inborn wisdom

- personal guide ... trusted counselor ... deepest friend

- treasure chest of love ... endless source of nurturing

- wellspring of inner peace ... serene place of silence

- true center ... grounded core ... real self

- dependable home ... truest identity ... innermost being

The soul is where ...

- we experience the beauty and wonder of life

- we see into the truth of every human being

- we are one, totally one, with all life

- we taste and experience life's deepest truths

- we meet, embrace and support everyone and everything

- we feel the divine living, resting and loving – within us

- we remember ... everything ... yes, everything

The soul is our source of ...

- *power* – to heal anything in ourselves and others

- *authority* – to take charge of ourselves, each moment

- *love* – for ourselves and for others ... unconditionally

- *truth* – to know everything we need to know, anytime

From within the soul, we can ...

- hear, feel and experience all life: divine, human and earthly

- know who we are ... what we are ... why we are ... where we are

- honor all creation, including and especially ourselves

In conclusion, the soul is ...

- the real, authentic you

- available to you at every moment

- inviting you into your truth daily

- nurturing you continually

- empowering you endlessly

What is the soul? Simply put, it's who you are! It's the real you!

Every time I re-read the above words, something stirs in my core. I feel deeply and freshly touched. I re-experience the beauty of this loving resource that daily nurtures all of us from within and from without. Its infinite power becomes a bit more tangible and feels even more available.

4

And in my experience with thousands and thousands of people, I've seen that down inside the soul and the human heart of the individual is a core of radiant love.

JOHN F. DEMARTINI[6]

The body is like clothing for the soul.

GEMARA SHABBAT[7]

In the greatest confusion there is still an open channel to the soul. It may be difficult to find. … But the channel is always there, and it is our business to keep it open, to have access to the deepest part of ourselves.

SAUL BELLOW[8]

It carries the majesty and wonder of life into my heart more palpably. Its all-knowingness stirs noticeably in my depths, inviting my own deep-seated wisdom to sample its truths more fully.

In short, soul to me has become one of the most awe-inspiring miracles of life imaginable. It's a treasure chest of pure love that generously nurtures, liberally empowers and wisely guides us beyond measure. Like the best of gifts, it keeps right on giving; it's available to you and me every moment of every day.

Soul gives to us, in fact, from every possible angle: through the unsought words of a cherished friend, through that unexpected "aha" in our mind, through those sudden, unanticipated turns in our external life, and—perhaps best of all—from the very dependable center of who we are.

Soul, I deeply believe, is the central, core self that you and I are. Our mind, personality, outer trappings—everything else is our soul's wondrous external expression, just as a painting is the tangible expression of the artist's purely inspired soul. While those exterior manifestations deserve our celebration and committed involvement, we also have the unique privilege of being the very life force that inspires them—that is, being soul—full-time.

That's why I've chosen to write this book: to afford soul the opportunity to share with you and others its vast wisdom and visionary truth … invite you to taste its inspiration within your own heart … and move you to experience your own soulfulness more fluidly and personally.

WHAT DOES THE SOUL SEE?

The short and simple answer is: the soul sees everything. Deep within ourselves—where our real, soulful self lives and reigns—you and I see everything, know everything and love everything.

Even when you're in the midst of a hurtful argument or a deeply painful moment, for example, the soulful you is—believe it or not—deeply in love with your adversary. That soulful self instantly knows the bigger reasons for the distressing event and is generously inviting you to its insightful perception and wise inner counsel. Ah, if we would but listen and attune to this internal warehouse of wisdom, we might save ourselves hours of needless anguish!

From your sacred, soulful perch above the forest of life, the soul-centered you sees the bigger picture of every event in your life—its inventive creation, its symbolic meanings, its rich invitations and its magical possibilities. You, deep in your soul, know the utter perfection of every circumstance and are deeply at peace with every aspect of life—your own life and that of the world.

In this book, I'm about to share with you a soulful vision of life itself. Not only does our soul see every aspect of life clearly, it views each aspect with a wisdom that, when we become aware of it, can make a tremendous difference in our lives. When observed through the soul's inspiring perspective, life comes alive for us. We open to life's miraculous qualities, and living it becomes an exciting adventure. When we are soulfully engaged with life, it feels more and more like a sacred ceremony, a gift-filled ritual of loving, learning and living. We feel blessed.

People travel to wonder at the height of the mountains, at the huge waves of the seas, at the long course of the rivers, at the vast compass of the ocean, at the circular motion of the stars, and yet they pass by themselves without wondering.

ST. AUGUSTINE [9]

THE SOUL'S STORY OF LIFE

Humans have been asking questions about the nature and purpose of life for centuries: Who are we? Why are we here? What's it all about? When we look soulfully, we notice that many answers have been offered over the millennia, and each offers its own singular, distinctive point of view. Religious interpretations, for example, often look different than philosophical explanations, scientific responses are sometimes at variance with societal ones, and our various cultural theories frequently don't mesh with our personal beliefs. Every version of life is unique, each having its own liberating advantages and, of course, its built-in limitations.

Perhaps the most important question for us is not, "Which answer or vision is right?" Rather, we might more wisely ask, "Which one stirs my soul, excites my heart, sparks my own deepest wisdom, and speaks my innermost truth?"

This book presents, of course, a soulful vision of life. In the following pages, I offer you an interpretation of these ancient questions, as I have been privileged to view them through the soul's visionary outlook. This soulful, mystical and inspiring worldview hopefully will ignite your own soul's equally inspiring wisdom and bring it more fully into your awareness.

It is the soul's duty to be loyal to its own desires. It must abandon itself to its master passion.

REBECCA WEST [10]

For me, this vision is not just a beautiful philosophy, it's alive as a real and practical part of my everyday experience. When translated into daily life (the focus of Chapter 5), it can dramatically expand our self-concept, draw us markedly back into our fuller resources, instill in us a profound level of inner peace, and support us in living a truly empowered and rich existence. While I did not write this as self-help book or as a means of offering you "how-to" pointers for living, I do believe that you will find many immediate and useful applications of this soulful vision to your own life.

As you read each chapter, you'll notice that I give this vision at least four distinct forms. First, each chapter starts with a scriptural perspective—this time-honored style is my way of honoring the beauty and sacredness of the soul's expansive vision. Next, the human perspective translates the vision into tangible, concrete terms for your deeper understanding. Then, the personal perspective invites you to apply the vision spiritually and personally into your own life. Finally, the inspirational perspective offers you affirmative sayings for your everyday motivation.

Let's begin the vision then. I invite you to read what follows with an open heart, receptive mind and engaged soul. I join you in a shared experience of what has been for me a sacred encounter, mystical journey and exciting adventure. May it be even more than that for you!

There is no need to run outside
for better seeing,
nor to peer from a window.
Rather abide at the center of
your being. ...
The way to do is to be.

LAO TZU [11]

ESSENCE: BEFORE THE BEGINNING

1

Everything we know stems from our own essence—indeed from the very essence of life. Just as the invisible yet powerful nucleus of an atom inexplicably holds and supports the immense creative activity of its electrons, so the unobservable but mighty force of infinite essence infuses itself into and supports everything that lives. This invisible, continuous source—the veritable power behind all existence—feeds and sustains us every second of our lives.

I've created the following scriptural portrayal of this remarkable phenomenon called essence to invite us mythically into its unique majesty and mystery. As you know, the cherished scriptures of our many cultures and religions so often communicate in the language of myths—the symbol-rich stories that speak inspirationally to our heart and deeper consciousness. Myths constitute a sacred expression of life's larger truths and, in this instance, the soul's inspiring vision.

THE SCRIPTURAL PERSPECTIVE
The Mysterious World of Essence

In the beginning, there was only essence. At that infinite point, before time began, there existed only source ... only being ... only the latent force that lies beneath and behind all potential. This presence was—and remains—the very *is-ness* of life that we have come to call God. In the beginning, time and space were not yet even imagined. Nothing was expressed, nothing set in motion, nothing visible, nothing created.

Yes, before the dream called life took form, nothing existed except this boundless, infinite, yet totally unexpressed power—whole and complete within itself, embracing all that could ever be. It needed nothing and depended on nothing for its existence. This essence of life, in its simple nature, contained everything, knew everything, was

There is no end to the details of My manifestation. I am the Self ... seated in the hearts of all beings. I am the beginning, the middle and also the end of all beings. ... I am the seed of all beings. There is no being, whether moving or unmoving, that can exist without Me. ... Whatever being exists, whether glorious, prosperous or powerful, know that it has sprung from but a spark of My splendor. ... I stand supporting the whole universe with a single fragment of Myself.

BHAGAVAD GITA[1]

everything. All possibilities were subsumed in and knew themselves only as the unexpressed God—absolute essence.

The only name neutral and simple enough to reflect the indescribable nature of this unfathomable essence of life is *That Which Is*. Long before the conception of time or space, *That Which Is* was the one all-encompassing and all-sustaining reality. All-knowing and all-powerful, it contained the potential to do and accomplish anything. Yet, it chose—mysteriously—to do nothing, express nothing, achieve nothing. It chose simply to be. *That Which Is* was a simple state of *is-ness*—not one of acting, creating or thinking. Such was that infinity before the amazing dream of life began.

Then, it happened. In an unpredictable act of creative dynamism, *That Which Is* began to express, to create, to manifest, to imagine. A dream-like space was imaged into aliveness ... and filled instantly with light ... which in turn created energy and consciousness. In that infinite act of creative inspiration, *That Which Is* expanded to become *That Which Lives*. In the limitless possibilities of this dream-like world, space and time came into imagined existence ... essence took on diverse apparent forms ... multiple dimensions and perceivable universes developed ... and God was now expressed in and through every created form.

Indeed, ever since the dream of life began—in and through time and space, energy and movement, and all human existence—that original essence has continued to thrive and express at the center of every life form. That same *is-ness* resides powerfully and fully within all its creations, at their very core—infusing them with its vital force and daily inventing life anew.

At that innermost center of life and within every human being, this unique essence dwells in all its indefinable mystery and majesty. This intangible yet primary power pumps the heart and moves the awareness of every human being. It constitutes the indescribable yet central influence behind every thought, impulse and activity. It is the humble yet mighty servant of each person's existence ... holding them together ... inspiring their consciousness ... propelling them at every turn.

Even to this day, at the depths of awareness, every human being can find that essential source of all life—infusing itself into their body, mind and soul—every minute of every day. It is accessible, touchable and available to everyone. In truth, that original self-contained essence—*That Which Is*—is your essence as well.

The gods Umvelingangi and Uhlanga gave birth to Unkulunkulu, the Zulu creator and Ancient One. He grew up in the reeds of a mythical swamp called Uthlanga in the sky and when he became too heavy, fell to earth. He then created the people, cattle, mountains, snakes, and everything else. ... He was the first person and is in everything that he created.

ZULU CREATION STORY[2]

Your essential nature is not at all in time or place, but is purely and simply in eternity.

MEISTER ECKHART[3]

THE HUMAN PERSPECTIVE
"Created in the image and likeness of God"

The scriptural account of creation above, as well as its longer version in the Prologue, offers us a simple but radical interpretation of our created nature. It tells us that the life-giving spark didn't just remain the original generative source "up there" somewhere, creating us as something separate from itself. Instead, it shows us that our inventive source—the all-knowing, all-powerful essence that imagined all life into existence—remains an ongoing and dynamic force. That essence is an alive and involved presence at the center of every manifestation. The very is-ness of life is our is-ness; it's who we are at the very foundation of our existence.

Given our more limited historical perspectives about creation, it may seem quite remarkable to envision ourselves as an embodiment of our creator, as a living expression of that essence. The story in *Genesis,* the first book of the Hebrew Scriptures, reminds us of this when it tells us that *"God created humanity as his image: as the image of God he created ... them"* (Genesis, 1:27). That seemingly simple statement gives us a major hint about our created nature—that divinity lives in our humanity. Yet, how many of us have grasped its profound and far-reaching meaning ... or put it into creative expression in our daily lives?

When we look deeply into this biblical statement—and into the creation accounts of countless other traditions—we start to see that everything that exists contains and expresses the very essence of the divine. How could it be otherwise? Even from a simply logical perspective, if everything was God before creation, then everything that emanates from God would naturally be filled with the very same divine nature, that same essence.

What does that mean about you and me? It implies that *we embody essential divinity* in our innate, created nature. This remarkable fact may or may not mean that you and I are everything that we conceive God to be—we'll leave that question to the philosophers. Consider this, though: while no single drop of seawater is as vast as the entire ocean, in a fundamental and real sense, every drop contains the identical make-up as the ocean itself. The ocean pours its very spirit and life force—its essence—into each drop of water within it, and every precious droplet is alive with the wonder and power of the ocean.

In the beginning there was endless space in which nothing existed but Tawa, the sun spirit, who gathered the elements of space and added some of his own substance, thereby creating the First World.

HOPI CREATION STORY [4]

God made humanity in his own image.

GENESIS [5]

*What, you ask, was the beginning of it all? And it is this ...
Existence that multiplied itself
For sheer delight of being
And plunged into numberless trillions of forms
So that it might find Itself ...
Innumerably.*

SRI AUROBINDO [6]

We appear on Earth as separate beings with diverse destinies; but as each separate raindrop is a part of the sea, so are we each a part of the Ocean of Awareness, the Body of God.

DAN MILLMAN [7]

From Wakan Tanka, the Great Spirit, there came a great unifying life force that flowed in and through all things—the flowers of the plains, blowing winds, rocks, trees, birds, animals—and was the same force that had been breathed into the first man. Thus all things were kindred, and were brought together by the same Great Mystery.

CHIEF LUTHER STANDING BEAR [8]

The universe emerges out of all-nourishing abyss not only fifteen billion years ago but in every moment. The foundational reality of the universe is this unseen ocean of potentiality. If all the individual things of the universe were to evaporate, one would be left with an infinity of pure generative power.

BRIAN SWIMME [9]

There is an image of God within each man; once seen, he will forever after court union with it.

PAUL BRUNTON [10]

In the same way, you and I are infused with the life force, indeed the very essential nature, of our divine source; that essence lives powerfully in and as us … and creates us anew, endlessly.

GOD'S ESSENCE … OUR ESSENCE

Describing our own essence is, of course, a difficult task. Essence, after all, is what's left after we remove every distinguishable quality. Once we eliminate every noun and adjective that defines us—including our name, appearance, profession, accomplishments and beliefs—only our is-ness, or natural self, remains. And that is-ness plainly cannot be described, defined or expressed. It simply is … we simply are … you simply are.

It's the same with infinite essence. If we choose to look past the many attributes that we assign to God—embracing love, compelling power and inventive creativity, for example—then we see a divine source that simply *is*, nothing more, nothing less. Indeed, this divine essence remains the power underlying every creation. When we are able to see beyond its many observable attributes, we find it to be the invisible, intangible force that radiates and glows at the very core of our lives.

We all share that same essence. We are all dynamic expressions of life—with every gift of love, power and creativity that accompanies that life—and we also are grounded in a simple yet radiant essence. At the depth of you and me—at the center of the storm of life—there lies a core and central self wherein *we just are*. In that quiet inner space, we have no concern about whether we're employed, well-liked or successful. We simply are who we are—with no adjectives, no descriptors. That's right. At the level of our soul, where our most innate, real self serenely resides, each of us is nothing short of mighty, foundational, grounded essence.

Here, at this central place of our own is-ness, we are most truly "created in the image and likeness of God" … we can find and live in a state of inner peace … we can see life through the visionary eyes of God … and we can daily celebrate and treasure life's beauty and mystery.

WHAT DOES IT MEAN?

What does it mean to be made in the image and likeness of the divine, to hold that essential spark of life as our center? Most fundamentally, it means that this all-creative spark lives not only in the infinity of space, but also meaningfully here in the three-dimensional world—in our own heart and soul. It means that this divine presence vibrates and resonates within you and me, as an intimate part of our daily experience.

We possess in our core what different religions call a God-Self ... a soul ... a spirit ... an indwelling divine presence ... the Holy Spirit. That remarkable imprint of life that many people call God—but please name it in whatever way creates meaning for you—is always alive and well in our innermost fabric. Our infinite source is active, involved and present in our depths and center. God's essence lives and breathes as our essence. When we breathe, we take in and exhale that universal breath of life. When we create our lives, we allow that pure essence to spark itself into dynamic expression, through and as us.

We've come to refer to that special phenomenon as our *soul*, a simple yet elegant term for that mystical center of humanness in which the imprint of the divine holds us in a deep and profound embrace. Simply by having a meaningful relationship with our soul, we're automatically united with the source of our being ... with our deepest truth ... with the ultimate essence of life. Imagine that. We have continuous access to this essential source—right inside our own uniquely created self.

Picture what it would be like if each of us somehow miraculously accessed that soulful self, connected with that infinite presence, and even became fully unified with that internal center of life—every day. What doorways would open to us! Possibilities would unfold before us, and hidden powers would manifest in and through us. Our potential to live dynamically and fully would be boundless, just because the unlimited power of that intangible source is also our power. We need only tap into it—into our own soul—to participate in its marvels and gifts.

Many holy persons throughout the millennia have had just such experiences. They have dedicated their lives to living in a deep communion with their souls, in loving oneness with God. Some have spent many hours and days in prayer, contemplation or meditation. And they have found God—within themselves.

As a result, their lives have been wondrously enriched and their daily experiences dramatically transformed. Many of them have found profound inner peace, rich personal happiness and marked human fulfillment—all because they have daily tapped their human selves into the fountain of their creative source. I'm not just referring to our recognized models, like Jesus, Buddha, Lao Tzu and saints from numerous religious traditions. Many modern persons who live and work

There was something containing all. Before heaven and earth it exists. Tranquil, incorporeal, alone it stands and does not change. Before heaven and earth had taken form, all was vague and amorphous. Therefore it was called the Great Beginning.

TAO TE CHING [11]

There is only one journey. Going inside yourself.

RAINER MARIA RILKE [12]

How quiet it is! Yet it can transform all things.

LAO TZU [13]

It is only with the heart that one can see rightly; what is essential is invisible to the eye.

ANTOINE DE SAINT-EXUPÉRY [14]

The essence of oneself and the essence of the world, these two are the same.

JOSEPH CAMPBELL [15]

Everything that exists has Being, has God-essence, has some degree of consciousness. Even a stone has rudimentary consciousness. … Everything is alive. The sun, the earth, plants, animals, humans— all are expressions of consciousness … manifesting as form.

ECKHART TOLLE [16]

Then the divine Self-existent … appeared with irresistible creative power, dispelling the darkness. He who can be perceived by the internal organ alone, who is subtle, indiscernible, and eternal, who contains all created beings, and is inconceivable, shone forth of his own free will.

MANU-SMRTI [17]

in our midst also actively pursue an inner calling to quiet soulfulness, inner groundedness and empowering centeredness.

Ironically, though our souls embody this source and invite us to it regularly, much of the time we barely notice it. We understandably focus our primary attention on our daily roles and responsibilities. We frequently define ourselves in terms of external, ever-changing attributes—our profession, status, family and social roles … our prized beliefs, principles and values … even our moods and emotions. We may come to believe that we *are* those characteristics and gradually lose touch with our innate identity, our inner home, our real self—our essence.

We simply don't remember to look within, unwittingly neglecting our relationship with our spirit. We forget that our soulful source is the most basic, intimate and natural part of our being … and that its presence and invitations are available to us every day. Consequently, we often miss the many blessings and gifts that await us in that inner core of our essential nature.

THE ROLE OF ESSENCE

What are those gifts of the soul … the blessings of our essential self … the fruits of an intimate connection with our divine nature? I've come to believe that our essence holds four special qualities and offers them to us every minute of every day. These important gifts, quietly and unobtrusively presented to our heart, are profound *truth,* sage-like *wisdom,* loving *non-judgment* and inner *peace.*

• Truth

First and foremost, our soulful center holds the real truth about us, in its purest and most essential version. It is where we sense, even know, the truest nature of our self, the fundamental meaning of our existence, and the clear purpose of our life. Here we can access the most core, simplicity-centered reality about ourself and intuit the most reliable inklings of our deepest identity. Quite simply, when we're connected to our innermost core, we know who we are and why we're alive.

That knowing doesn't usually translate directly into the concepts of our conscious mind, however. It's a deeper knowing that gives us a larger vision and allows us a fuller grasp of who we are than can the more limited ideas of our trained mind. Rooted in the wonder-filled mystery of life, it usually speaks to our mythical, intuitive sense and expresses in a special language that each of us can easily learn: the language of essence.

Yes, essence has its own language, one that is neither logically-based nor rationally-centered. To learn it, we need only sit quietly and pay attention ... with our mind still, our expectations silenced and our focus open. Yes, we need only let go of the regular thoughts and preoccupations of the day, sit silently in the middle of our being ... and simply be. *Simply being* is rather easy, actually: we just stay open-minded and receptive. We do nothing, attempt nothing, think nothing and expect nothing. We just *be* in the moment, remain alert, stay open and allowing, and notice. In this state, the language of essence speaks itself into our inner consciousness—without words and without fanfare. Then, all of a sudden, we notice that we know ... and have little need to translate that knowledge into the language of the conscious mind. We're content to know without explaining or expressing it. How delicious, how delightful, how simple!

• Wisdom

Our essence is also an inner reservoir of fuller vision. From here, we can look at life through the wisdom-filled perception of our heart, rather than through typical human eyes—ones that are conditioned to see only observable information. Here in our all-embracing heart, we see life in its infinite perfection, instead of viewing its assumed imperfections. We access and connect to life's beauty, our own beauty and the beauty of every person who surrounds us. Here we profoundly understand the deeper meanings of life's dilemmas and find the wisdom-filled possibilities hidden in its dramas.

Many of us are quite attached to our perceptions of imperfection—whether in events, others or ourselves—and cherish our beliefs that the world is a mess. While these perceptions and beliefs may seem harmless, our adherence to them cuts us off from the deeper truth that resides in our all-knowing core. They keep our central wisdom hidden—just because we're tuned in to a different, commonly shared channel of awareness.

It's quite natural, you know, to find that inner wisdom. All we need do is look at life, or any aspect of it, and ask our heart the simple question: "What is the wisdom in this situation?" Then we stay silent for awhile ... and listen ... in the quiet spaces of our depths. And we wait, for a brief moment or sometimes for days at a time. During that wait,

Just meet here, where silence is— where the stillness inside dances ... where you touch the eternal ... where you want nothing, and where you are nothing. ... Meet here where you find yourself by not finding yourself ... where quietness is deafening, and the stillness moves too fast to catch it.
ADYASHANTI [18]

Being is the eternal, ever-present One Life beyond the myriad forms of life that are subject to birth and death. However, Being is not only beyond but also deep within every form as its innermost invisible and indestructible essence. This means that it is accessible to you now as your own deepest self, your true nature. ... You can know it only when the mind is still, when you are present, fully and intensely in the Now.

ECKHART TOLLE [19]

Only the heart knows how to find what is precious.
FYODOR DOSTOYEVSKY [20]

14

*We are God dreaming
that we are not God.*

DON MIGUEL RUIZ [21]

*Your vision will become clear only
when you look into your heart.
Who looks outside, dreams.
Who looks inside, awakens.*

CARL JUNG [22]

*It is life nearest the bone where it
is sweetest.*

HENRY DAVID THOREAU [23]

*The aim is ... to realize that
one is that essence; then one is
free to wander as that essence in
the world. Wherever the hero
may wander ... he is ever in the
presence of his own essence—for
he has the perfected eye to see.*

JOSEPH CAMPBELL [24]

*It is enough that one surrenders
oneself ... to the original cause
of one's being. Do not delude
yourself by imagining such a
source to be some God outside
you. Your source is within
yourself. Give yourself up to it ...
seek the source and merge in it.*

RAMANA MAHARSHI [25]

we simply stay open to hearing a message, feeling an intuitive sense or seeing a bigger vision—no matter what, even if it seems to contradict our treasured biases, assumptions or beliefs.

An example from my own life may illustrate this point. In my early adulthood, I spent an extensive period bemoaning my childhood circumstances, grieving over the belief that I never received the love that I needed from my family, and generally resenting my parents deeply. In short, I was feeling enormously sorry for myself and blaming my family for my misery.

Then, one day, it occurred to me to follow the sage advice of the preceding paragraphs. So, I sat myself down and asked the deepest levels of my soul this question: "What is the real truth, the bigger vision, the actual wisdom in this scenario?" Rather quickly, I heard a clear and unexpected inner voice, expressing authoritatively and strongly, "The problem, Bill, is that you are a disappointment as a son!"

I was astonished and amazed. These words carried an interpretation that I had never even thought to consider. It took me awhile to let their deeper truth fill my understanding, but I really got the message. I had spent so long feeling disappointed by my parents that it never occurred to me to see how disappointing I had been to them. I wasn't a good fit in that family, and everything about me was out of step with their values, ideas and orientations. I finally saw how difficult it had been for these two precious people to raise me, and how every expression and action on my part must have hurt them.

Gradually, I began—for the first time ever—to feel real compassion for my dear parents, to understand them from my heart and to genuinely feel their pain. Over time, I let go of my petty hatred, self-serving biases and narrow-minded self-pity. As more time passed, I accepted my parents as the wondrous expressions of life they were, and ultimately came to feel a deep and authentic love for them—all because I decided to invite the fuller wisdom of the situation to speak to me.

• Non-judgment

In this special center where the essence of life reigns, we hold absolutely no judgments, no criticisms and no condemnations about ourselves, others or the world around us. Our soulful center is that unique "eye of the storm" from which we see the higher truth of life and experience the growth-oriented invitations of every circumstance—often in interesting contrast to the perceptions and opinions of our everyday conditioned thinking. Without the usual disparaging judgments, justice-based criticisms and negative interpretations, we're free to see life's multiple options, make more creative choices, and enjoy our daily experiences.

It's so easy—as well as tempting, socially acceptable and drama-producing—to find fault with and condemn ourselves, others or life. Yet, nothing in our essential self has those tendencies. At our core, we see only the pure truth of any person or situation. At this deep level of clear vision, we set aside the psychologically or societally based biases that inform our regular interactions ... and we see only the beauty, deservingness and lovableness of what we behold.

The great Mohandas Gandhi (The Mahatma) demonstrated non-judgment powerfully. No matter what atrocities he observed the British colonizers committing against the Indian people throughout the 1930s and 1940s, he consistently refused to utter a negative or condemning word against them. Even during a brutal war in which the British were his official enemies, he committed himself to love and honor them, refused to hurt or kill them, and called upon the Indian people to show them love and kindness. This approach of total non-judgment comes from the pure love of the heart.

During one phase of my life, my wife Donna and I owned a treatment center for persons, mostly children, with learning disabilities. As you know, "learning disabled" (note the label) children have quite a difficult time reading and/or performing other academic tasks because their brains and minds function differently from those of most other students. Also, as you can imagine, they are often and regularly the object of significant negative judgment on the part of their teachers, and even jeers and taunts from their peers in school. The implied message: something's wrong with you ... you have a problem ... you're not acceptable.

Because I had the opportunity of interacting intimately with these children, viewing them through their own eyes for several years, I watched my judgments about them undergo a deeply felt shift. I began to see their style of learning not as a problem but as simply a unique and different way of learning. I also discovered research that decidedly interpreted the problem not as a learning disability but as a teaching disability—meaning that often school systems simply didn't have the flexibility or vision to help these students learn in their own ways.

There is nothing wrong in the universe. Wrong exists in our limited view of the universe.
THE KEY [26]

Conflict arises from living in ways that do not feel correct for you. Sensitively attune to your inner being and allow it to lead you. Then your own life force ... can guide you on life's path.
ALEXANDER AND ANNELLEN SIMPKINS [27]

If the doors of perception were cleansed, everything would appear as it is, infinite.
WILLIAM BLAKE [28]

A little wise secret: You don't need to know anything in order to be wise. All you need to do to be wise is to accept.
THE KEY [29]

The ego looks for what to criticize.
But love looks upon the world
peacefully and accepts. The ego
searches for short comings and
weaknesses. Love watches for any
sign of strength. How simple it
is to love, and exhausting it is
always to find fault. ... Love
knows that nothing is ever needed
but more love. It is what we all
do with our hearts that affects
others most deeply. ... We love
from heart to heart.

MAHARISHI MAHESH YOGI [30]

All that we see or seem,
Is but a dream within a dream.

EDGAR ALLEN POE [31]

Accept as a principle that there
is nothing to attain, because
what we are looking for, we are
already ... every step you take to
attain yourself is a going away ...
there is nothing to gain, nothing
to lose ... you will find yourself,
naturally, as you were before you
were born.

JEAN KLEIN [32]

So, whether it's an opinion about learning disabled children, or some aspect of ourselves that we've not accepted with love, or someone who is a true thorn in our side, there's a good chance that the problem is not with that person or situation but with our own judgment about it.

To paraphrase an old Buddhist saying: just because you don't like something doesn't mean there's anything wrong with it. It just means that you don't like it.

Amazing things happen when we let go of a disapproving or condemning judgment. We begin to see the apparent conflict from a different perspective *(truth)*, we find a fuller vision *(wisdom)* that guides us into a new relationship with it *(non-judgment)*, and we begin to feel an inner calm *(peace)*—all of which allow us a completely new set of options in relation to what earlier had felt so challenging.

• Peace

Fourth, and perhaps best of all, our soulful center is a space where we can find a true and lasting sense of *inner peace*. It's the refreshing oasis where we can drink the pure waters of truth and rest in the embracing shade of serenity. The closer we move into the love-filled circle of our essence, the more we discover life's innate okayness, even its rightness, and let go into the truth that everything is just fine as it is.

I find it striking that we are often so busy trying to change so many things in and about our lives. Especially in an age where we are schooled in the importance of focused intention, envisioning, goal setting and decision-making—all of which have great benefit when applied masterfully and pragmatically to our lives—many of us have forgotten the other side of that coin: how to find the meaning and perfection in "what is."

We've conditioned ourselves to keep changing aspects of our lives, with the hope that we'll be happier and more fulfilled if this or that is different. In fact, it often is important to make these dramatic changes in our lives—if and when our soulful truth is the wise source of that inspiration. In contrast, however, I've spent many hours with hundreds of people who have forgotten how to find that inner guidance. As a result, they are on a non-stop merry-go-round of changing the external circumstances of their lives—jobs, relationships, neighborhoods and so on—yet they never feel the promised happiness at the end of the ride.

What would happen if we embraced whatever circumstances came to us, everything life offered, with an attitude of acceptance, receptivity and welcome … rather than trying to push it away or change it?

My own experience with this approach, as I've practiced it over the years, has been this: I made friends with the difficult situation rather than resisting it as unwelcome. I spent precious, if usually painful, time listening to its deeper meanings, when it would have seemed more comfortable to ignore it. And I opened myself to its hidden invitations instead of hiding from what it might be asking from me.

As a result, I found that something shifted in me—without my having to change the external situations. I let go of long-held narrow attitudes, out-of-date judgments, left-over feelings of smallness, and old emotional wounds. Best of all, I gradually found a state of inner peace. In contrast to my earlier habit of non-acceptance, I experienced total okayness with what was presenting itself to me, and an appreciative embrace of its gifts.

When we look out at life from our sacred inner space of essence, we have no alternative but to feel unified with the infinite, all facets of life and ourselves. In this realm of loving non-judgment and expansive vision, personal peace reigns supreme. It's a true blessing—and it's all ours.

Our essence is an intimate, integral part of our make-up. It's who we are, our real self—and it never leaves us. Even if we have touched and been touched by this internal center only once or twice in our lifetime, it is always there, alive and well at our core, just waiting for us to snuggle into its truthful, wise, non-judgmental and peaceful embrace.

CINDY'S STORY

I once had the privilege of mentoring a forty-five year old woman named Cindy. A devoted single-mother of three children, Cindy had juggled motherhood and work in an exceptional way. Highly respected in her career, she had achieved a significant level of success.

Cindy came to me at a time of personal crisis. Her children were finally out of the nest, and her life was theoretically hers once again. Yet, she found herself suddenly without direction, focus or purpose. Having given her all to her children, devoting her life to them and their well-being, Cindy had indeed lost herself.

When you don't cover up the world with words and labels, a sense of the miraculous returns to your life that was lost a long time ago…. Things regain their newness, their freshness. And the greatest miracle is the experiencing of your essential self as prior to any words, thoughts, mental labels, and images.

ECKHART TOLLE [33]

Do you hear a voice whispering in the background of your busy life that seems to be calling you to some mystery? Subtle but always there, a presence that you sense is somehow your real essence. If we really let the voice of our soul and its connection to the universe flow into us, what will happen?

SANDRA COSENTINO [34]

If a plant cannot live according to its nature, it dies; and so does a man.

HENRY DAVID THOREAU [35]

I first asked her to tell me what she needed. Her response took me a bit by surprise. "I need a new self," she proclaimed.

"A new self?" I asked. "Would you tell me what happened to your old self?"

She proceeded to do exactly that. "Well, my old self has just been dying off the past three years. And in the last few weeks it seems to have totally died. Everything I've lived for is gone, and I feel completely empty inside. With my kids grown, no man in my life, and no purpose to give myself to, nothing means anything to me, not even my job. I've been wandering around aimlessly … and I'm feeling all alone. It's a really scary place to be."

I understood. Like many of us, Cindy had lovingly centered her life around others and her heartfelt obligations to them. She hadn't taken time to nurture herself, let alone to know herself, during all these years. Now the moment of truth had come: it was time for Cindy to find meaning and purpose within herself, and she hadn't built the inner foundation to do so.

I asked her to tell me what she saw or felt when she was alone with herself, when there was nothing and no one around except her real self.

It is the soul's duty to be loyal to its own desires. It must abandon itself to its master passion.

REBECCA WEST [36]

"You've stumped me," she said, with a look of pained bewilderment on her face. "Whenever I'm by myself, all I can do is look for some kind of distraction—I read, do projects, even aimlessly clean my already clean house—anything not to face the dark emptiness that's lurking inside me."

I explained to Cindy what was happening. I described how her soul, which holds the truth and plan of her life in its all-knowing intelligence, had just turned off the meaning that had been sustaining her earlier sense of self. It was now inviting Cindy to enter into a fresh phase of living—with a new life purpose and style of fulfillment. I told her that now her life needed to be built on a different foundation, one based on her own truth rather than that of others.

Cindy looked a bit puzzled, but asked me to continue. "In a huge and major transition like yours," I suggested, "you can't just shift automatically from one life purpose to another. First, you need to get to know yourself, your real self—deeply and intimately. It's only when you have a strong connection with your soul, your inner truth, your core self, that you can discover the bigger plan for your new life."

All things in the world come from being. And being comes from non-being.

LAO-TZU [37]

Well, Cindy took my lead. She knew that she had moved beyond her former sense of identity, and that none of her old tactics worked anymore. More importantly, she realized that something deep inside was calling to her, and calling strongly. Finally, she was eager to discover what it was.

So, we got to work. I asked Cindy to spend time each day "just being" with the empty, dark space deep within her. And she did. Every morning and night she spent twenty minutes forcing herself to be with her emptiness and hang out in the seeming nowhereness of her inner being. It wasn't easy at first to face her fears. She had to learn to find a previously unknown source inside herself that would protect and accompany her in this dark space.

Shortly, to her surprise, the darkness began to dissipate and the emptiness slowly took on a new form. Cindy gradually started to feel the beginnings of life stir in her. This different and unexpected experience seemed a bit strange at first, but then began to be, well, quite natural and pleasant. In her words, "I felt like a part of me that had been buried under layers and layers of obligation could finally breathe … and it was starting to move in me."

Cindy now felt a small degree of confidence and hope, so we moved on to the next step. I asked her to start talking to this newfound part of herself, asking questions like, "Who are you?" and "Do you want or need anything from me?" Again, she did so with an enthusiasm and commitment that was palpable.

When I saw her next, Cindy told me that she was having regular and sweet conversations with her "inner self." What she was really excited to tell me, though, was that she had made a unique discovery. "I've found my real self," she announced, "my own soul, the honest-to-goodness true me!" With a look of wonder on her face, she continued, "I've finally found the beginnings of who I am, and, you know what? I really like this me!" I was happy for Cindy. She had just come home to her soulful self, to her essence.

Over time Cindy found a deeper and more intimate relationship with her essence. She discovered a source of love within her that nourished her tenderly. As a result, she no longer needed to look outside of herself for nurturing. She also found a repository of truth at her center and was able to tap into its guiding wisdom whenever she needed it. In addition, Cindy discovered a place of actual peace—because she was now living daily in an inner home that met all her needs.

Try to discover your true, honest, untheoretical self.

BRENDA UELAND [38]

True salvation …is to 'know God'—not as something outside you but as your own innermost essence. True salvation is to know yourself as an inseparable part of the timeless and formless One Life from which all that exists derives its being.

ECKHART TOLLE [39]

ESSENCE AND YOU

You and I, of course, are tapped into the very same essence as is Cindy. It's at our center, just as it is at hers. *That Which Is,* with all its divine attributes—all the love in the universe, all the power in the world, and all the creative vitality of life—thrives in the core of our own human selves, as well as in the far reaches of the cosmos. Best of all, like Cindy, we can access those divine qualities, claim them and celebrate them as our own—because they are already an intimate part of each of us.

Please take a journey with me now—a journey into the budding magnificence of your life. First, envision the same essence that exploded into the creative form of the universe actively residing within the inner sanctum of your heart. Imagine yourself not only aware of that internal essence, but centered and grounded in its limitless gifts. Picture yourself just as connected to the treasure chest of your soulful center as you are to the externally compelling dynamics of your life. See yourself walking through your day guided by your deepest source rather than being primarily moved, shaped and absorbed by external circumstances and events.

What does that life look like? Can you picture yourself always in touch with this profound source of truth that dwells in your core? Can you envision feeling free to speak from that truth in your relationships and interactions, instead of saying what you think people want to hear? How does it feel to see yourself acknowledging and expressing your soul's purest vision, rather than echoing ideas that only vaguely reflect your deep inner knowing?

Here's the final question: What would your life be like if you lived firmly centered in your soul, in essence, all the time? My sense is this: you would feel more aware of and connected to your own truth. You would hear the voice of your soul's unique wisdom more clearly and be open to letting it guide and inspire your life in both small and big ways. Most of all, becoming increasingly one with your soul, you would feel more and more like the person you were truly created and intended to be. You would feel so natural and whole. And finally, you would indeed find yourself living with remarkable inner peace, joy and fulfillment.

THE PERSONAL PERSPECTIVE
Finding Your Own Essence

How do you open yourself to a deeper connection to divine essence, not just as that infinite source "out there," but also as the internal resource that lives in your core? How do you establish an intimate bond with the indefinable is-ness that occupies that essential space within you? How do you unify with that infinite spring of life that is not only the limitless creator of the entire universe, but also the very foundation of your own soul?

Of course, every person will answer these questions in his or her own way. There probably are as many paths to oneness with our essential self as there are people populating our planet, and we are unlikely to find one single style or method of unifying with God's indwelling presence. As different as we all are—and should be!—each person's relationship with God and life must be unique.

Nonetheless, to help you find that often-elusive connection to and embrace of the God Within, I offer you a five-step approach that has been useful to many people. I invite you to try it, if you choose, and then feel free to change it to meet your own needs and style.

Here I dwell
Within the midst
A neutral zone
A place soul-kissed

No opinion,
Either good or bad
No feeling
Happy or sad

Just being here
I find my Self
My essence true
A transparent hue

Transcending all
Yet within it too.

HEIDI HALL [43]

STEP ONE: GOING WITHIN

- First, remind yourself that God—or whatever name you use for that creative spark—really is present inside you … that the divine truly lives not just *in* your core, but also *as* your core … that your nature is absolutely sacred. Feel free to repeat these words several times, as a soft and gentle mantra: "God's essence is my essence. My nature is divine! I now touch the sacred within me!"

- Now picture yourself sinking or melting into that divine center … gently taking your place in your sacred core … entering into the divine presence of your source as it lives in your soul.

- As you experience yourself leaving your external focuses behind and uniting with your quiet internal center, observe what happens. Quietly witness that indescribable sacredness within. Feel it welcome you into its midst, and open yourself to the sacred presence of essence.

STEP TWO: CLAIMING YOUR DIVINE NATURE

Now that you have touched the God within, invite yourself to claim that divine source as your own nature. Having merged with infinite is-ness in your own soul, take the next step—owning that ultimate essence as your own.

- Remind yourself that your core and depths are totally, totally divine … that you are everything God is, just as each drop of water contains the ocean's essence … that you have every right to claim infinite essence as your own.

- Express or repeat, as you feel moved, words such as: "My divine essence radiates out and moves through all the layers of my person. It radiates through my feelings and emotions, my mind and thoughts, my words and actions, and my relationships and friendships. I am completely filled with divine essence, as it suffuses me with its light, love and power. Just as the sun shines its light into our solar system, splashing its radiance onto each planet, so the light of God that exists in my center blesses every facet of my being. I claim that light, that love and that power as my own."

STEP THREE: EXPERIENCING INTIMATE CONNECTION

You have let go into the embrace of your divine center and have claimed this center as your truth. Now invite yourself to enter into an intimate relationship with that divine essence as the most fundamental part of you.

- Imagine yourself in that comfortable internal space, sitting right next to God, about to have a private conversation with your divine source. Remind yourself that this is not happening anywhere outside you, but rather as an intimate part of your own experience. How miraculous it is that this source has expressed not just in and as the vast universe, but also in and as you!

- Just as you relate naturally and honestly with a dear friend, do so now with God dwelling in your soul. Look at your divine creator as your best friend, as your unconditionally loving parent, as your devoted guide, as your most ideal self—in short, in whatever way allows you to feel safe, intimate and trusting.

- Begin talking. It mostly doesn't matter what you say; simply express whatever you feel moved to communicate. Just let yourself pour out your feelings, thoughts or desires. Continue talking until you feel done.

- Now, listen. First, listen to the silence ... to the emptiness ... to the depth. Then, listen to the unspoken response ... to the quiet wisdom ... to the nonverbal inspiration. Finally, listen to the subtle message ... to the intuited answer ... to the sensed truth.

STEP FOUR: LETTING YOURSELF BE LOVED

Any intimate interaction between close friends includes that miraculous phenomenon called love. It's time to open yourself to being loved by this divine source, intimately and deeply.

- Give yourself permission now to be loved unconditionally—yes, absolutely unconditionally—by your innermost source, who has been waiting at your core all these years to give you this ultimate gift—unconditional love. If taking this permission fully into your heart proves a bit difficult, help yourself by saying these words: "God created me perfect, sees my beauty and knows my divine nature. I open myself to being loved by my creator, now, just as I am. I deserve this love, receive this love, and become this love."

- Picture yourself opening your heart, just like you would open a window to let in the light of day. See the love that has been waiting for you, hovering in front of your heart. Take this special moment to look at that love closely. Notice its tenderness, its softness, its gentle caring. It's the unconditional love of life.

- Now, let this sacred love into your depths. As it pours into your waiting heart, drink it in, receive it fully—don't deny yourself its loving blessing. Notice how it feels, how it touches your emotions, how it immediately begins to heal your inner wounds. Allow yourself to feel loved, held, embraced, nurtured.

- Finally, just sit there for a time, bathing in this infinite love, feeling God's transforming touch, and simply letting love happen. Don't think about it, just experience it.

As you know, most of us find it easier to love than to be loved. Our deep-seated self-judgments or feelings of unworthiness and shame usually allow us to take in only a fraction of the love, both human and divine, that is sent our way. For these few moments, though, set aside your self-doubts or feelings of unworthiness and let love do what only love can do—make you feel whole.

STEP FIVE: SIMPLY BEING

Have you ever noticed how some couples who have been married for a long time often just sit together without talking? They seem to share special moments of love that don't require the usual styles of communication. The truth is, they enjoy simply being together and have somehow learned to convey their love in simple, profound and nonverbal ways. It seems that their essence has taken charge of the interaction.

- Just be. Just be. After any communicating that you have just done internally, give yourself time now just to be—to hang out in essence without any words. Simply sit and enjoy the divine company that lives forever and invitingly in the space called "you."

- In the silence, in that sacred place of just being, notice what's happening. Out of the seemingly empty spaces, gradually, almost imperceptibly, you will be filled with a gentle sense of intimacy … of oneness with your source. Just be with this subtle phenomenon, without thinking about it.

- Finally, express gratitude in whatever way is genuine to you. Thank that divine source and essence that lives as your soul for the experience you have just had and the blessings you have just received.

That's it. That's all you need to do. Each time you tap into your own soulful center in this way, you're more connected with its many gifts. As you leave the experience, ask yourself when you want to return. If you want to, feel free to make a date with your soul for another time. You can look forward to something special and real.

THE INSPIRATIONAL PERSPECTIVE

At the end of this and each subsequent chapter, I've felt moved to include some special sayings to help you recall an underlying wisdom and apply it to your life. You may use these as personal affirmations, helpful suggestions or meaningful reminders.

I lovingly offer these "points to remember" so you may take them into your reflective mind and open heart in whatever way helps you to find your own deeper truth and inspiration. Also, know that you have my full permission to copy these pointers and refer to them regularly in any manner that supports you.

If you are looking for a daily practice, I invite you to consider this one: take five minutes each morning—perhaps before you go to work or begin your regular activities—and read slowly and contemplatively through the following affirmations. Allow each saying to move gently into the deeper realms of your mind and touch you in the quiet places of your heart. Let them inspire you, then move you into that essential place of your own knowing. Finally, just sit for several seconds in the silence, allowing these truths to settle into your depths, so they may speak to you throughout the day. Then, move gently into your day.

This brief practice may also be used as a wonderful nighttime ritual. Relaxing into your very essence in the precious moments before falling asleep can be a powerful influence in creating more meaningful and peaceful hours of sleep.

So, I invite you now to read through these expressions of deeper truth in a way that is inspirational and motivational to you.

- My innermost self is host to the essence of all life. How privileged I am!

- Everything in creation expresses God's wonder and perfection—and so do I.

- When I spend time with my soul, I am sitting in the sacred temple of the divine.

- God lives in my center … and is with me all the time, including right now.

- When I listen to the quiet voice of my soul, I can hear life's loving whisper.

Each of us possesses an exquisite, extraordinary gift: The opportunity to give expression to Divinity on earth through our everyday lives. When we choose to honor this priceless gift, we participate in the recreation of the world.

SARAH BAN BREATHNACH [44]

- The divine is fully present in every creation. It is present in me too—right now.

- I'm created in God's image and likeness. My essence holds the blueprint of all life.

- Essence created me as a reflection of its limitless wonder. I am wonder-full!

- Life's love and grace are always there for me. I open myself to receive them—now.

- I am a vibrant expression of God. In me lives everything I need for an astounding life.

- The creative spark lives fully in my heart. I can spend special time there every day.

- I am made of the same stuff as the stars. I am a brilliant, radiant being.

- In my essence lies a peace that fulfills all my needs. I unite with that peace now.

- My essential self sees the perfection and beauty of everything in life. I embrace it all.

- Life is amazing and wonder-filled. I claim the vision to see and celebrate it all.

- I now blame no one and find fault with nothing. I am my all-loving essence.

- I see only truth—the truth of myself and everyone else. We're all perfect "as is."

- I am a wise, all-knowing self at my core. I claim that wisdom for my life—now.

In my experience, only pure Being or 'Isness'— the infinite, immoveable stillness that precedes creation—exists. It has no knowable content and yet it feels absolutely full.

Like a divine magician, Being appears to become an endless and ever-changing variety of forms that we call creation.

We tend to get thoroughly fascinated by and lost in the forms and forget their essence or Being.

Yet all those forms and appearances are like a dream for when we wake up from the dream of creation, we find only Being.

CYNTHIA LANE [45]

LET THERE BE LIGHT!

THE SCRIPTURAL PERSPECTIVE
From Essence to Light

That Which Is began to evolve a most unusual thought: What would it be like to experience the qualities that are dormant within my essence? What if my is-ness were not only a state of being but also an external expression? Divine essence imagined this possibility as real and, in that instant, created a dream-like state in which it could see, experience and revel in all its infinite qualities.

Thus, the dream began—and a remarkable dream it was! At the very beginning of the dream an extraordinary thing happened. God said, "Let there be light!" And immediately, appearing as an awe-inspiring, explosive extravaganza, *That Which Is* burst forth into manifestation—as light.

Light instantly filled the void and created a vast universe, completing it with a luminosity, brilliance and power that had never before been known. Light magnified itself and spread to fill every possible space with an unspeakable brightness. This glorious light was so dazzling and powerful that nothing else could be seen. All existence was boundless, endless, luminescent radiance.

In this wondrous dream, God assumed a truly marvelous and spectacular form—as an awe-inspiring light, a glowing force that knew no bounds. As light, the dream contained the very essence of life but manifested it as luminosity. Accordingly, this exquisite light possessed all the power of the divine—the power to create anything, transform anything, magnify anything, penetrate anything. Yet, for a brief but precious moment, the infinite was content only to shine brilliantly and to fill the virgin space with total splendor. This unending light was totally self-contained, self-fulfilling, self-generating—an amazing sight to behold.

Let there be lights in the expanse of the sky to separate the day from the night, and let them serve as signs to mark the seasons and days and years, and let them ... give light on the earth.

GENESIS [1]

The universe was in darkness …
There was no glimmer of dawn,
no clearness, no light, and then
Io began by saying these words,
'That he might cease his state
of inactivity.'

Darkness became a light
possessing darkness, and at once
light appeared.

Io then repeated these words,
'That he might cease his state
of inactivity.'

Light became a darkness
possessing light.

A third time he spoke, 'Let
there be one darkness above
and one below. Let there be one
light above and one below …
a domination of light, a bright
light.'

And now a great light prevailed.

MAORI[2]

The dream continued to evolve as, soon, another remarkable event occurred. Divine essence chose to express itself further—no longer just as grand, boundless luminescence, but now in other unique and expressive ways. Thus, the dazzling light of *That Which Is* took the form of individual lights that we have come to call stars. Each brilliant star retained within itself not only the vast radiance of the universe, but also the infinite quality of divine essence—the all-powerful being and essence of the creative source.

As time passed, long and barely measurable, amid the uncountable trillions of light-studded stars, infinite light gave birth to a small but quite special star that became known as the sun. This radiant star continued the divine creation by sending fragments of its luminous self out into the space around it. These light fragments swirled, collided and united—and took on an entirely new form, that of planets. One planet, earth, became the ever-evolving, ever-creating home to it own diverse versions of light.

The dream of creation had now evolved to the point of even new possibilities. The luminescent sun unleashed, from its limitless reservoir of universal potential, two unique and special gifts—and infused them deeply into earth's developing fabric.

The first of these infinite gifts was ongoing creation, or *creativity*. The light's boundless capacity to create itself into unlimited expressions became an intimate part of earth's nature. Creativity was now this planet's special destiny. Thus, through eons of time, earth continually created and recreated herself, generating geologic shifts, both great and small. Continents joined and separated; islands emerged and disappeared; mountain ranges rose and fell; tectonic plates shifted; oceans advanced and retreated. Earth constantly reinvented herself through ever-changing physical and biological expressions.

Innumerable life forms manifested and passed away, and newer ones arose. The earth brought forth an immeasurable variety of plants, flowers, trees, fish, birds, reptiles and mammals, including human beings. Yes, human life, and indeed every life form on the planet, now mirrored and embodied light's vast imagination, remarkable creative nature, and constant capacity to change. So it was that God's essence became light, and light became earth's ongoing creative force. And so it remains today.

The second gift that infinite light bestowed upon this new planet was *love*. From the beginning, love became an intimate ingredient in earth's intrinsic composition, infusing itself into each of her developing creations. Indeed, all earthly creatures—human beings, animals, plants, even rocks—are created not only in light's creative genius, but also in the mysterious and magical quality of love. All life on earth is imbued with love's unique and life-giving capacity for inter-connectedness, relationship, intimacy, bondedness and unity. And to this day, love is a powerful, influential and moving force of life—indeed, one of light's most dynamic expressions—on this small planet that encircles that special star called the sun.

THE HUMAN PERSPECTIVE
We're Light Beings

Our present day physicists teach us that all material elements of the universe—including our bodies and the buildings in which we live—originate from nothing other than stars, that is, light. According to this scientific perspective, as well as the worldviews of many ancient spiritual traditions, each of us is a continued expression of that first, enormous flash of divine brilliance. From all these angles, it's clear that we all are "light beings."

Granted, we often don't see ourselves that way. Most of us have become quite attached to viewing ourselves and our world as primarily material creations. But that doesn't change the underlying truth that everything and every one of us is made of, influenced by and propelled into our daily lives with light. Indeed, light is our ever-present generative source—we are filled and resonate with its wondrous luminosity, every minute of every day. It feeds our nervous system, infuses itself into our brain waves, inspires our thoughts, and generates our very life force.

Can we see light? On quick reflection, many of us might answer with an automatic "No!" However, as we peer more deeply into the question, we find ourselves moved to an increasingly compelling, "Yes!" Let's explore light's intriguing visibility.

When you look at a friend across the room, you generally focus on that person, taking no notice of the seemingly empty space between you. In fact, though you may not be consciously aware of it, there is a vibrant field of light that is literally alive between you and the person you're observing. Your mind automatically negates or ignores this dynamic field of light that holds you and your friend, so you can see the other person clearly. In truth, however, you are looking at, as well as through,

You can forgive a child who is afraid of the dark. The real tragedy is when men are afraid of the light.

PLATO [3]

In modern science, everything that exists in the world is energy. Light is energy, and everything, at its root, is light. In the Toltec tradition, the information carried by the light is called the silent knowledge, and all of us are vessels of the light.

DON MIGUEL RUIZ [4]

A field that transports light … and replenishes the energy lost by atoms and solar systems is not an abstract theoretical entity. No wonder that more and more physicists speak of the quantum vacuum as a physically real cosmic plenum.

ERVIN LASZLO [5]

The
Earth
Lifts its glass to the sun
And light —light
Is poured.

HAFIZ[6]

Now, is it a surprise to discover
that 99 percent of your body's
substance is nothing, empty of
visible, material substance?
And that nothing is the
'substance' of 99 percent of this
universe? Is this the scientific
way of saying you are spirit?

K. C. COLE[7]

It is ... a fairly astounding notion
to consider that atoms are mostly
empty space, and that the solidity
we experience all around us is an
illusion.

BILL BRYSON[8]

a rich light field whenever you focus your attention anywhere outside, or even inside, yourself. Light is inescapable—it's everywhere we look, it's everything we are, and it's everything that connects us.

This dream-like space that we call human and earthly existence is created by and filled with an omnipresent field of effervescent light. As described by physics, a field is a phenomenon that transmits or extends an influence over a large, even unlimited, amount of space, and anything that exists inside a field feels its effect. At this and any moment, you and I are actually living in an infinite, quantum field of light. Light is present everywhere in and around us, and propagates its influence through every detail of our lives.

It's true. Light, that very first and wondrous manifestation of the divine, holds us in its supportive embrace every minute of every day. It saturates our minds, sparks our thoughts, and infuses strength into our bodies. It is the hidden power behind everything we experience around us. Light has created us ... and continues to create us afresh, as it bathes us in its renewing and generative luminescence every minute.

OUR LIGHT-FILLED UNIVERSE

Today's pioneering scientists tell us that approximately 99.9 percent of the human body, of all matter in fact, is made up of empty space. Yes, 99.9 percent of the atom, the basic material building block of the known universe—including you and me—is actually empty, devoid of substance. From this perspective, the only seemingly solid part of the atom is its subtle, ultra-thin outer film, or surface. This is true of all atoms, whether we find them in our bones, our brains, a stone or a chair.

Strange as it may seem, that less-than-one-tenth-of-one-percent, shifting external border of the atom is all that gives our universe the appearance of matter and substance. The line between form and formlessness is indeed startlingly slim.

Astonishingly, however, our inventive, intelligent mind helps us out. Without skipping a beat, it subconsciously and continuously influences us to perceive people and objects as solid, simply by magnifying that one-tenth-of-one-percent of apparent matter into what looks like a consistently solid material being. What ingenious minds we have, to create such a convincing illusion! And now that we have discovered the illusion, let's turn our attention to our true nature—light!

Scientists have described the non-substantiality, or emptiness, that fills each atom in a number of ways: as space, vastness, pure potential and, most frequently, light. Ancient spiritual traditions, based on their gifted perceptual abilities, have consistently referred to it as pure *light*. No matter what label we choose to apply, this pervasive pan-atomic space that surrounds, fills and contains us is, in truth, a limitless field of primal, dynamic and vibrant light. It is—and we are—essence in action, creating ourselves anew every day as light.

Let's recap briefly. As the divine dream emerged, essence's first, all-pervasive surge into creation took a dramatic form—as an amazingly creative *light*. That first light of creation now permeates every corner of our universe. Everything that we observe has emerged from, is created by, and is filled with luminescent light. What we call space holds—and in fact *is*—an infinite light field; light permeates every manifest form and saturates every atom in every cell of every creation. In short, you and I are dynamic, vibrant, radiant beings of light!

SEEING LIGHT EVERYWHERE

This amazing creation of essence into light was not just a singular, historical event. It happens anew everywhere we look, trillions of times every day, ingeniously, all around and inside us. Essence is continuously blazing into light, filling the universe—including that microcosmic universe called you and me—with its ever-expanding, delightful richness. Its light ignites into daily expression in our brains and thoughts, our cells and sub-atomic activity, our emotions and energies, our relationships and involvements, and our accomplishments and achievements.

If we intentionally re-attune our natural sensitivities to this amazing phenomenon, we can actually begin to experience the light nature of our bodies, feel light's electrical workings in our minds, and observe its creative magic throughout every aspect of life.

Imagine what it would be like if we retrained our minds to perceive everything and everyone, including ourselves, as an embodiment and expression of light. How would it be if we saw the world as it really is instead of as the convincing tricks of our minds lead us to believe? What do you think would happen?

In addition to perceiving people's physical qualities, we would actually begin to experience their essential luminosity and radiant nature. We would see ourselves and others as literal embodiments and

The universe emerges out of all-nourishing abyss not only fifteen billion years ago but in every moment. The foundational reality of the universe is this unseen ocean of potentiality.

BRIAN SWIMME[9]

*I am a messenger of Light.
I am a pilgrim on the way
of Love.
I do not walk alone,
but know myself as one
with all great souls,
and one with them in service.
Their strength is mine.
This strength I claim.
My strength is theirs,
and this I freely give.
As a soul, I walk on earth.
I represent the One.*

ALICE A. BAILEY [10]

conveyors of light—to witness them not just as material bodies but also as bright and gleaming beings of light. Such an approach would radically change our everyday lives. It would bring us one giant step closer to the truth of who we are, and permit us to experience people—as well as ourselves, nature and, in fact, all life—as the amazing, awesome and wondrous creations that they truly are.

Are you willing to try a simple experiment? Look at someone now, either in person or in your mind's eye. Notice—or intuit, sense or feel— how their light extends outward from their body ... gently touches others ... and interacts supportively with the energetic environment around them. Stay with this approach for as long as you need to, even if at first it seems like your own imagination might be playing a role.

Now try seeing your own light doing the same thing—exuding from your center, manifesting your unspoken gifts, and carrying your heartfelt love into the world around you. In reality, of course, this is what is happening all the time, even though we've subtly programmed ourselves not to see it.

Certain people, usually those gifted with a unique spiritual vision, can actually view the light nature of everything and everyone around them. They see every individual and experience as a movement and expression of light. These unusually sighted persons sometimes share with us what they see: one person's light holding another in a loving embrace ... a beam of light emanating from someone's heart and taking rest in his or her mind to influence an impending decision ... two people's light bringing nurturing and healing into their shared pain, even in the midst of a mutually hurtful argument. Light is truly a devoted and powerful "behind the scenes" player in nature's daily display of creative activity.

You may or may not have that particular quality of vision—most of us don't. Nonetheless, it's heartening to know that each and every one of us is totally filled with this remarkable light ... and that light permeates every component of our physical makeup, every impulse of our minds, every wave of our emotions, and every space around us. Indeed, light is truly one of our best and most loyal friends as we negotiate our way through this challenging experience of earthly living.

OUR LIGHT NATURE

Quite naturally, we have always associated light with God and those who are close to God. Portraits of saints, angels and holy people from all faiths have frequently shown them surrounded by supernal halos of

We are not human beings trying to be spiritual. We are spiritual beings trying to be human.

JACQUELYN SMALL [11]

I see the first dream or expression of Being as a vast and brilliant light that I call FirstLight. As the initial manifestation of creation, FirstLight contains within itself the seed or potential for all that can be known or experienced, the total potential for creation. That astounding FirstLight is equally powerful, equally present and equally accessible in all of us.

CYNTHIA LANE [12]

light. Many ancient medical traditions have described light as the most powerful healing vehicle available to us. Sacred writings often describe God as using light to intervene and create miracles in the human scene.

Even modern medicine, though not necessarily linking it with divine properties, has avidly employed light's healing applications, such as laser-based surgery. In space-oriented science we measure universal distances in accord with the speed of light. In our modern movies, we view our space age heroes wielding light sabers, protecting themselves with light shields, and teleporting themselves through the supportive waves of the universe's light field. We innately know light's immeasurable presence and power.

As light beings, our light is equally powerful and sacred. Because we're created in the image and likeness of our divine source, that essential creative, dynamic power is fully present in us as well as all around us—in the form of our light. And that awesome light has the power to express and be experienced in so many ways and at any given moment. Expressed as light, what we call the omnipresent divine and creative source is totally unavoidable and wonderfully powerful!

We can access this remarkable light in countless ways—by sensing its radiance in the atoms and cells of our bodies, by imaging its electrical workings through our nervous system, or by intuiting its radiance in our etheric energy field, to name a few.

How powerful we would be if we intimately embraced this magnificent light that so overflows with possibilities within us! Wouldn't it be marvelously fulfilling to somehow make friends with our light nature, to understand its life-giving qualities more completely, and to open ourselves to its unexplored powers for healing, transformation and growth? Indeed it would.

In fact, you and I are already strongly experiencing our light's magic at the deeper levels of our awareness—physiologically, energetically, unconsciously and subconsciously. It's only at the conscious levels of our thinking processes—where we've simply forgotten to notice light's presence and possibilities—that we're not using, enjoying and celebrating this amazing aspect of our luminous make-up.

Perhaps it's now time to re-awaken our conscious awareness to this miracle of life called our light nature. If you agree, let's take that journey of re-awakening together.

Einstein discovered that the 12 major elements that are in our body are also present when a star is born. Science has discovered what ancient peoples always knew, we are literally made of stardust.

SANDRA COSENTINO [13]

You have within you the divine Spark—the indwelling Christ—and by awakening and developing this, your spiritual nature, you can mold conditions to fit your needs.

EMMET FOX [14]

MY PERSONAL EXPERIENCE OF LIGHT

About twenty years ago, something quite subtle but powerfully life-altering happened in my personal life. Almost overnight I started noticing—seeing, observing, interacting with—the awesome light that lives so vibrantly in people, nature and events around me. A new, albeit puzzling, gift had just been bestowed upon me: the gift of seeing and having an intimate relationship with light.

This new vision grew remarkably over time. Bit by bit, I found myself more and more united with this light, eventually becoming totally one with it. Ultimately, in the deepest core of my personal identity, I literally became the light—and experience myself to this day as a full embodiment of light. But let's start at the beginning.

At first, as you can imagine, I had no idea what to do with this newfound ability. So, I listened to my inner inspiration—and felt moved simply to observe the light that showed itself both in and around me, and to listen internally for any sense, signal or message about what I was being invited to do with this newfound connection.

Slowly, the invitations became clear. First, I felt invited to learn light's special language, which, I quickly discovered, is quite different from the language of our logical minds, our feeling-based energies or our verbal expressions.

I can't tell you exactly how I learned the unique language of light. The simplest explanation is that I remained open to it, neutrally witnessing the light, letting it fill me, then watching its mystery-sourced wisdom express naturally through my non-logical, non-feeling and nonverbal self. That's right, light spoke to me through a different channel—one that has no name or label, but that I can only call the light field or vibration that we all have and share. I slowly learned to interpret that light resonance, as it translated itself to me through my intuition, subtle energies, biological pulsings and essence-based knowing. Over time, I came to understand its wise movements, its creative styles and its loving language.

The second invitation, once I adequately grasped light's unique and subtle style of speech, was to participate in its creative endeavors as a cooperative, involved cohort ... to enter into an intimate partnership in the light's inspired ventures. No longer could I just be the neutral observer or the grateful receiver of our light's daily gifts. Rather, I was now being asked to step beyond my previous sense of separateness and

Sensitively attune to your inner being and allow it to lead you. Then your own life force, your vital energy, can guide you on life's path.

ALEXANDER AND
ANNELLEN SIMPKINS [15]

I am what is around me.

WALLACE STEVENS [16]

smallness to become light's collaborative arms and hands, its earth-based grounded tool, its human instrument of ongoing creation. Light seemed to want me to help it in its earthly creations and was asking me to be its human partner.

LIGHT'S AMAZING CREATIONS

What kind of creations, you might ask. Over time I sensed the light inviting me to participate in four kinds of creation here on earth:

- First, the creation of *healing*.

As you know, most psychological and energetic—and even many medical—healing modalities focus on the remarkable, awesome power of our mind and of our energy.

Well, I learned that light is its own dynamic and rich healing source—one that is actually much more powerful than the force of the mind or energy. I had long healed people with love, energy and/or consciousness as my primary focus, but now I was led to realize the vaster, grander, bigger healing capabilities of this phenomenon called light. And what a powerful healing force it is!

- The second creation is *transformation*.

Not only can our light heal our ills, it can transform literally anything. Just as the light of the sun easily transforms ice to water and water to steam, so the light of our nature can change any one form into another, in the blink of an eye.

For example, when we find ourselves needing a more solid inner strength, a firm and grounded base on which to build a newfound personal power, we can go directly to our light for help. We can invite light to change our old shaky or insecure inner foundation into a stable new one. Yes, light has the ability to not only heal our old woundedness or lack of self-confidence, but it can build a new foundation to take its place—and it can do so easily and quickly.

Also, when the time comes for an old habit to go—either a behavioral one like smoking or an energetic one like feeling sorry for ourselves—light can make that happen literally overnight. Light has the power to change any of its creations into new and different ones. After all, whatever styles we have were initially created by light, so light can easily un-create and re-create them into different forms.

The stars have the ability to assist in healing. For example, in the Navajo Great Star Chant, the stars of the sand painting on the hogan floor receive their healing power from a bright star that shines through the smoke hole in the roof of the hogan.

SANDRA COSENTINO [17]

Over time, light quietly tutored me in its natural styles of healing and transformation. It showed me, in one internal mentoring experience after another, how it tenderly wraps its loving light around the old habit or form, then—just as easily as the sun's rays melt ice to create water or evaporate water to generate steam—its powerful touch brings about the new creation, without needless process, flashy fireworks or energy-draining drama.

I was amazed and delighted at first that both healing and transformation could be done so easily, so naturally, so quickly. I had been trained as a psychologist in the often pain-filled techniques, processes and rituals of healing, yet had long felt that there must be a gentler, kinder way of growth. I found that new way in the simple, quiet and miraculous workings of light.

- The third of light's creations is *empowerment*.

We all need empowerment—the power, for example, to take charge of our minds, be in loving relationship with our emotions, generate positive health, and create our lives effectively. Light, that ever-resourceful expression of life's essence, can create power anywhere and everywhere, instantaneously. When we're connected with and, better yet, aligned with our own light—or the light of the universe—it automatically comes to the fore and volunteers to create whatever we need.

So, this expansive, omnipresent light taught me how it creates power. Over the years, as I've let light manifest this strength-generating creation through and from me, I've watched people become wondrously empowered emotionally, physically, mentally and spiritually—in their health, in their habits, in their relationships, and in virtually every aspect of their lives. And all this happened because the light came front and center, moving itself from luminous to focused, and splashed its gifts into the tangible lives of these special people.

- And the fourth creation, *enlightenment*.

When most of us think about enlightenment, we imagine holy monks or Eastern mystics meditating on a distant mountaintop. But I'm not referring to that external look of enlightenment here, enticing as it may be.

Rather, I'm addressing how each of us can bring our awareness totally into the light-filled—or en-*light*-ened—nature of our make-up. I've

Learn the craft of knowing how to open your heart and to turn on your creativity. There's a light inside of you.

JUDITH JAMISON [18]

From the viewpoint of light … nobody is enlightened, nobody is non-enlightened, everything is light. The direct path consists of taking this viewpoint and boldly staying there.

FRANCIS LUCILLE [19]

been privileged to help countless people become aware of and intimate partners with their own light and the light of everything around them. Truly, when we can sense, discern or intuit the light of life wherever we gaze, or perceive every aspect of ourselves as light, our whole experience of life changes forever. We naturally become deeply aware of life's beauty, celebrate nature's wonder, and stand in awe of everyone's magnificence. This fresh vision of life's luminescent grandeur is like seeing everything through the eyes of the divine. This experience may just be our own modern, perhaps more Western, version of enlightenment.

As you can imagine, once I became fully immersed in the light and mastered its creative styles, it was a short step to completely identifying with it. For you too, the first step, if you've not already taken it, is simply to open your consciousness to the light ... let it speak to you in its own language ... let it invite you in its own way ... and follow its mystical cues.

LIGHT IN ACTION

I've just described four modes in which light invited, and continues to invite, me to co-create with it in ever-expanding, ever-renewing, ever-purifying ways. Those descriptions imply that light is perhaps the most ingenious creative force in the universe. It can create anything ... and continue to create it, over and over, for millennia on end.

As a small example, this amazing light can craft our bodies anew on a regular basis—and, indeed, it already does so behind the curtains of our daily awareness, creating new cells and regenerating old ones minute-by-minute. According to the most recent scientific estimates, 600 billion of the body's cells die off each day, while the same number spring to life—ten million per second. Our skin cells live for only two weeks before dissolving forever and giving way to entirely new ones, while the cells in our bones regenerate about every three months.

What is the hidden force behind this astounding, ongoing, regenerative, creative act? In truth, it is nothing short of our very own inexplicable, consistent, dependable light.

Light also re-creates our etheric energies—our emotions, chakras and feelings—regularly transforming them and generating new energies. It renews our minds, expands our inner vision, creates unexpected possibilities for us—and can bring about unforeseen miracles in our lives.

One day the sun admitted,
I am just a shadow.
I wish I could show you
The Infinite Incandescence (Tej)
That has cast my brilliant image!
I wish I could show you,
When you are lonely or
in darkness,
The Astonishing Light
Of your own Being!

HAFIZ [20]

'Each second, some 100,000
chemical reactions occur in a
given cell.' These are ... 'a highly
controlled process in which the
light acts as the communicator
that makes the reactions happen
at the right moment and in the
right place.' ... [B]iophonic waves
resemble the focused light of a
laser beam.

URSULA SAUTTER [21]
QUOTING FRITZ-ALBERT POPP

I've been privileged to observe these miracles time and time again over the years. I've seen physical healings in which broken or curved bones have been instantly healed. I've witnessed emotional healings where a person's lifelong depression or anxiety vanished in a moment, never to return. I've observed people's etheric energies transformed on the spot, completely changing their energetic relationship with life, themselves and others. In short, light in action makes the word miracle quickly obsolete and its workings appear commonplace.

In my opinion, with light in our awareness we have come home to our true nature. As light beings we are led into life's fuller styles of being human. With light we can draw the higher—perhaps fourth, fifth and sixth—dimensions into harmony and unity with our three-dimensional human experience, bringing ourselves closer and closer to our natural, multi-dimensional selves. When we are connected intimately with our light, we feel more whole, more complete, more fulfilled, more fully ourselves.

LIGHT'S UNENDING GIFTS

Let's look more closely at what it means to be a being of light, a self whose basic nature is light. What does it signify for our lives that light wondrously fills everything in and around us? From my personal experience, I've uncovered five special effects of light's unseen but vital activity in our lives:

- Truth

First and foremost, light's presence implies that we can *know* the deeper *truth* about ourselves and about, well, almost anything. Light has lovingly woven itself into the invisible fabric of our soul—that personal space of our deepest knowing—in the form of clear truth and uncluttered wisdom. From that sacred inner source, with great devotion, it makes its pure truth available to us.

Here, deep in the treasure chest of our soul, we can experience our own innate truth as well as the deeper truth of any aspect of life. For example, we can access the truth that we are beautiful and dynamic expressions of a divine creative source ... that the very essence of *That Which Is* lives in us as our own essence ... and that we therefore share the same underlying perfection that we otherwise assign only to God.

Because light is the first expressive language of essence, it can lead us directly and dynamically to the purest truth of our own essence.

Where there is great love there are always miracles.

WILLA CATHER [22]

One cool judgment is worth a thousand hasty counsels. The thing to do is supply the light and not heat.

WOODROW WILSON [23]

Belief consists in accepting the affirmations of the soul; unbelief, in denying them.

RALPH WALDO EMERSON [24]

It magnifies our deepest knowing and amplifies the inner voice that whispers to us from the utter quiet of our soulful being. Because of light, we can clearly and confidently "know" what we know. Because of light, we can bypass the logical thought processes and learned problem-solving techniques of our rational mind, and rest confidently in the genuine truth of our soul's profound wisdom.

Further, we can discover another dynamic truth: that within us everything sparkles with infinite light and holds a powerful divine radiance—a radiance that we can experience personally. We are able to know that, because we *are* light, light's unending gifts are ours to cherish and use in our lives. Our innate beauty is one such gift that can lead us to appreciate and celebrate ourselves and others. Light also gives us the blessing of experiencing life's splendor, perfection and wonder every day, which allows us to join in that splendor and actually feel the ways it embraces and blesses us in our daily life.

- Divine Presence

Second, being made of light means that we can actually *experience the divine*—not just as a mental concept or belief, or as a presence "out there" somewhere, but as a radiant inner glow that we can feel. Indeed, our light invites us to participate in creation's brilliance by feeling its luminosity in and around us. Because all our cells, thoughts and feelings radiate and embody our divine source, through them we can literally experience our divine presence within us.

Infinite light is soaring through our bodies, minds and spirits every second of our lives, just waiting for us to perceive and become it. Not only can we know that we are divine, but we can have the vibrant, personal experience of it at any time.

In short, because of our light nature, each of us is, in our own unique way, a true mystic—a person who lives the divinity of God as fully as the humanity of life.

- Freedom

Third, being light offers us the joy and privilege of feeling *free.* The more we realize our light nature, the more we give ourselves permission to behave as light—flowing freely, moving naturally and soaring easily. We can gently drop our sense of heaviness and seriousness, feel less defensive and self-protective, and take ourselves and our life circumstances, well, more lightly.

Be ye lamps unto yourselves.
Be your own reliance.
Hold to the truth
Within yourselves,
As to the only lamp.

GAUTAMA SIDDHARTHA [25]
THE BUDDHA

Any profound view of the world is mysticism.

ALBERT SCHWEITZER [26]

Freedom is the essence of who you are. Freedom is the essence of love. The word love *and the word* freedom *are interchangeable.*

NEALE DONALD WALSCH [27]

If you really want to be free, you've got to be prepared to lose your world—your whole world. If you're trying to prove your world view is right, you might as well pack your bags, and go home.

ADYASHANTI [28]

Light may one day be used to prevent disease. For 30 years, German physicist Fritz-Albert Popp has been working on experiments that are revolutionizing medicine. His research shows that at the most subtle level it is light (energy) that determines the state of health of the human body.

URSULA SAUTTER [29]

Indeed, we can begin to notice and enjoy the myriad ways in which light invites us to personal freedom. For example, we can release our learned and beguiling guilt—for light knows nothing about our seeming imperfections and blames us for nothing. We are able to embrace ourselves more positively as wonder-filled embodiments of divine radiance, and bask daily in the freedoms that such a self-concept allows us. More and more, we can claim personal freedom as a joyous life style.

After all, light's imperative is to invite us back to the more pure, clear and simple version of life that was intended for us here on earth. We can actually feel light's permission to perceive this planet anew, to see it just as it was described in the scriptural account of the Garden of Eden—as a place of joy, freedom and de-light. Yes, a personal experience of light can change our whole relationship to this precious planet of earth/Eden on which we live, ushering us back home, where the heart reigns supreme!

• Healing

Fourth, having light as our nature invites us to relish its transformational and *healing* qualities. As we know from modern medicine's love affair with laser surgical procedures and full-spectrum light techniques, light-centered healing is easier, gentler and more immediate than the more mechanical, traditional methods—and it's much more powerful and effective.

This dynamic characteristic of light can heal not only our bodies and their symptoms, but also our troubling emotional difficulties and complex mental illnesses. Light, because of its simplicity and power, cleanly cuts through the layers of our learned pain and brings our deep levels of suffering to their natural state of equilibrium and balance—without the need for belabored historical processes and pain-filled approaches

As light beings, we are born with a powerful tool that can heal any aspect of ourselves and our lives easily, quickly and effortlessly. What an amazing resource our light is!

• Oneness

Fifth, and perhaps most important, when we look at life through the unique lens of light, the apparent separation between people fades and the inherent *oneness* of the human family and, indeed of all life, becomes clear. Just as we can see a jigsaw puzzle as either a collection of individual pieces (duality) or as a comprehensive and integrated image (unity), looking at the puzzle of life through the eyes of light allows us to see the whole, unified picture of everything—without the distraction of the lines between the pieces, without the personal and collective pain that results from feeling separate and isolated.

Oneness has been called our natural state by many sages and spiritual traditions throughout the ages. They imply that, while we have developed our perception to see and react to life's creations—such as persons and events—as though they are independent and separate from one another, the bigger truth is that we are all interrelated, interconnected and integrated facets of life's unified and mysterious field of activity.

Knowing ourselves to be intimately linked and interdependent—bound together in a coherent state of oneness—instantly changes our experience of other people. We start to see every person not just as living his or her own life, but also as a radiant mirror of our self and our life. We understand that another's circumstances are but a reflection of our own, even though they may appear different from ours on the surface. We begin to understand others more easily, identify with them more fully, and feel a more genuine and tender compassion for them.

Yes, with light as our perceptual guide, we can easily find that illusive sense of oneness with every aspect of life ... and wondrously enjoy its life-changing benefits.

With this fivefold blessing of being a light-filled self, why would we pretend that we are anything other than light? With light as our nature, does it make sense to continue believing that we're primarily a materially-based person who doesn't have the freeing gifts of light at our disposal?

The fact is, since God lives as light in our bones—and everywhere else in and around us—it is our birthright to own and enjoy the rights and privileges of this beauteous light nature.

Larry's Experience of Light

A middle-aged man named Larry, in his first appointment with me, confided, "I've been having some strange experiences lately, and I'm hoping that you can help me understand them." I asked him to tell me about what was troubling him.

The good news is that we are all one. The bad news is only a small minority of us realizes this. Most of us are asleep in the nightmare of separateness. And the misguided conviction that we are separate from each other is the cause of untold suffering. It is the root cause of all our individual troubles. ... [T]he only solution is to wake up to oneness.

TIMOTHY FREKE
AND PETER GANDY [30]

We eventually become aware of our unity with the whole because it's inescapable. The awareness is wired into us, because we're wired into the universe. We can try ... to pretend we're separate from the rest of the universe, but one way or the other it will catch up to us and welcome us back into its embrace.

GAY HENDRICKS [31]

I was aware of a radiance emanating from a place I knew nothing about, a place which might as well have been outside me as within. But radiance was there, or, to put it more precisely, light. ... I felt indescribable relief, and happiness so great it almost made me laugh. Confidence and gratitude came as if a prayer had been answered. I found light and joy at the same moment, and I can say without hesitation that from that time on light and joy have never been separated in my experience. I saw light and went on seeing it though I was blind.

JACQUES LUSSEYRAN [32]

"Well," he slowly explained, "I've always been an ordinary guy living a normal life, though deep down I have felt somewhat different from regular folks. But about a year ago, I started having, well, some really different kinds of experiences."

Sensing that Larry needed some reassurance that I was comfortable with what he was about to share, I told him that I've had and witnessed a lot of "outside-the-box" aspects of life, and that I thought I'd be able to understand.

He continued more confidently, "Well, I've had what must be out-of-body experiences, where I suddenly found myself—I mean my spiritual self—hovering above my physical body just observing what was going on. For some reason, I wasn't afraid at all; in fact, it all felt perfectly natural and normal ... until I came back into my body. Then, as soon as I looked back on the experience as me, Larry, the physical person, I started to freak out."

I asked Larry to tell me more of what he observed when he was hovering over his physical self. He appeared relieved finally to have someone in whom to confide, and eagerly continued.

"Well, the whole experience was really interesting. It seemed like I was floating in this field of light ... like a cloud of light was simply holding me in its invisible arms. Then, I started to see myself really differently than I usually do. As I watched my human self lying there, I saw my life through different eyes, in fact, through the eyes of the light that was holding me."

"What did you see, Larry?" I asked him.

"It was like my life passed before my eyes—I mean, my new eyes, my spiritual eyes. I saw myself walk through my whole life all over again, but this time I saw how everything that had happened was actually perfect. Would you believe it? I even saw all the traumatic events as just right, exactly what I needed at the time, like they were given to me as a gift. It really blew me away, especially after how much I've cussed and complained about them, and blamed myself for making terrible decisions."

I started to ask Larry another question, but he gestured for me to let him keep talking.

"Now, Bill, I have to tell you the best part. Well, I don't know if it's best or not, but it completely confused me. I saw myself—me, Larry—as *perfect*. There I was, looking at my body, and all I could see was total perfection. It was like nothing was ever wrong with me, or even could be. More than that—now get this, Bill—I couldn't find anything wrong with anyone else either! They were just as perfect as I was. It was like we were all mirrors of each other's wonderfulness."

He continued, seeming more sure of himself. "And something else, truth be told, I've never been much into this God thing, but I felt God's presence inside me and all around me. The very same light that was surrounding me was also *in* me—and in everyone else around me. I saw it; I actually saw it."

"You said it was confusing. What was confusing about that for you, Larry?" I asked.

"Well, first of all, who could I ever tell that I am perfect, that nothing is wrong with me? Nobody would believe me. Come to think of it, how could I ever tell anyone else that they're perfect?

"Second, I've never had a thought like that about me or other people, ever. I'm perfect, just as I am? Come on, now, Bill. How can even I believe that? The funny thing is, though, that this crazy sense—that I'm okay, all right, filled with light, perfect—has stayed with me, even kept me up at night. It won't go away … won't let me forget it."

I realized by now that Larry had little experiential or conceptual background to help him understand his recent mystical experiences. So, I proceeded to support him in assimilating his new gift of light: the gift of seeing the real truth about himself and life—the truth that we're all created perfect. I guided him more deeply into the truth of his perfection, affirming his new way of seeing himself and his life through the lens of his light nature. Then, I helped him to understand that, rather than making him crazy or weird, these experiences were a beautiful gift, simply lifting him to a higher, fuller, clearer level of perception.

Then I asked, "Larry, why do you suppose this new knowledge won't go away? Why does it want you to keep remembering your perfection?"

"Well," Larry mused, "I've given that a lot of thought. It seems like I'm being asked, hmm, maybe even called—and I really hate that word—to do something with this knowledge. I don't know what, just something. That's all I know."

Again, I felt moved to offer a thought. "I wonder, Larry, if this outside-the-box experience and its new vision are asking you simply to hold this new knowledge in your heart for awhile, and then spend the next few months absorbing it into your 'regular mind.' After that, it may serve as the foundation for something else that will someday become clear to you."

Larry felt intuitively that my words rang true. I saw him again from time to time following that first meeting. Over the next many months, he not only got more comfortable with his newfound sense and experience, but gradually brought his human perceptions to that same plane of light that had earlier influenced his knowing. He even trained himself to view himself, his acquaintances and his life circumstances through the mind-expanding eyes of that gift-giving light. Most important, Larry was beginning to love the feelings of inner peace and joy that this new gift brought to him.

When I last saw Larry, he had digested the implications of his experience and was fully enjoying his now grounded perceptions of perfection. He was gratefully looking forward to wherever his newfound grasp of truth would lead him.

LIGHT AND YOU

Larry's story shows us the revolutionary power of light. His experience helps us see how our light reveals to us the bigger truth about ourselves, the truth of our innate perfection, both personally and collectively. Unlike Larry, though, we don't have to wait for some extraordinary phenomenon like an out-of-body experience to initiate us into this truth.

We can simply decide now that it's time for us to have the same connection with light that Larry did, though perhaps without the drama attached, and invite it into our lives. We can intend that the light will call us to our version of that same perception—that everything and everyone are perfect just as they are, including us—and open ourselves to the unfolding of that experience in our awareness.

The following section may be of help in opening our lives to the utter miracle of light.

THE PERSONAL PERSPECTIVE
Becoming Light

You and I are born and made of light. It's totally natural for us to know and experience ourselves as light beings and to use our light to heal and dissolve our problems. It's our nature to let our light go out and touch those around us, heal their pain, and hold them in unconditional love. As a being of light, it's our right to see ourselves through the unifying lens of light, feel our innate wonder, and embrace our God-given perfection.

Light is truly the most phenomenal and exciting aspect of our human selves. We can know fully that we are light. Why should recognizing and living this be complicated? It's not. In fact, it is as de-*light*-full as it sounds.

Who are you as a light being? I believe that you are someone who has the innate potential to express your love, power and truth in dramatic and singular ways. I believe that, to the degree that you identify with your light nature, you can truly move mountains, heal diseases and overcome any and all personal obstacles. I believe that, as someone who realizes his or her light nature, you can enjoy the freedom and ease of a life that you can finally experience as wonder-filled and perfect. Yes, light is that powerful, creative and rich. It is, after all, the primary expressive force of God, and God can do anything.

How then can you actually experience your light nature as well as the light in everything around you? I've devised the following five steps to help you connect with your "lightness" and live in its wonder-filled gifts.

Think of yourself as an incandescent power, illuminated perhaps and forever talked to by God and his messengers.

BRENDA UELAND [35]

STEP ONE: SEE YOURSELF AS A LIGHT BEING

- In your mind, picture yourself as a radiant being of light. Release any tendency to focus on your seemingly material quality. Instead, when you envision your body, mind or emotions, see them only as a sparkling light. If it's helpful, recall that at least 99 percent of your body's atoms are filled with light.

- Sit with the above picture for awhile. Give yourself permission to get comfortable with it. As you're enjoying seeing your light body, feel free to say to yourself, "I am light" or "I am a being of light." This mantra will be like background music echoing the truth of your light nature into your deepest levels of awareness.

STEP TWO: DISCOVER YOUR PERFECTION

- In the midst of the above mantra, open yourself to your light's truth. Invite your light to reveal to you the truth of your created nature.

- Ask the light, "What am I?" or "Who am I?" Listen quietly, internally for the answer. Keep in mind that it might appear immediately

We come,
As Beings of Light
Quantum essences
Stellar, bright

Light moves through our energy
To heal
Powerful quality, to congeal

A new story, entwined
With woven threads of
Light Divine,

Whatever we dream,
Comes into being

From struggle to free,
In this cosmic
Journey.

HEIDI HALL [36]

or come slowly over time. Either way, the response might sound something like this, "You are made in my image and likeness." or "You are perfect." You could also hear or intuit something like this, "There is nothing wrong with you." You might also hear or receive an understanding that as light you can now accept yourself just as you are.

- Of course, many, many other responses might show up, because your light is individualized and expresses through and as you in unique ways. And, the internal answers might change over time as you increasingly identify with your light nature.

- Once you ask, you will definitely get an answer. Be open and alert so you can recognize it. Your answer can appear at any time and in many ways. It can come all at once and immediately, or gradually, in parts, over a long period. It might take the form of an internal thought or insight, but it could just as easily be something that you hear in a conversation, a line that jumps out at you from a book or a movie, or a common experience that you perceive in a totally new way. You may not fully understand your answer at the moment it comes—deeper, richer meanings may reveal themselves to you as time passes.

STEP THREE: PUT LIGHT TO WORK

- Let light move through you. In the first two steps, you pictured yourself as light and asked yourself who you are as light. Now, you're inviting the light that you are to "go to work," to reveal itself in ways that are natural and easy for it. Ask the light to manifest itself in and through you.

- Ask the light to express itself in whatever way is natural and right for this moment. For example, if you have a particular illness or problem, ask the light to demonstrate its healing capacities by entering into and filling the space of that condition or issue. You can also ask the light to express itself powerfully to resolve a nagging question, or to open your mind to a bigger style of thinking.

- Believe. Believe that the light, in its capacity to do anything, will give you this gift. In "Step Three" in the last chapter, you gave yourself permission to be unconditionally loved. Now apply that willingness to be unconditionally loved by asking the light to express itself in a tangible way that you can experience. Be patient. Hang out with your light. Watch (or feel) the light wash through you as it effortlessly accomplishes your intent.

STEP FOUR: IDENTIFY WITH LIGHT

• Now that you have opened yourself both to be light and experience light, call yourself to identify even more completely with the light. Know that when you do this, you are embracing God in a fresher, stronger way.

• Say to yourself, "I am the light of God, and I invite myself to be taken over by that light, to be incorporated into that light, to become that light. I invite my human self to know its light nature completely and to become totally absorbed into that light." After all, since you truly are light, why not invite your consciousness to catch up with that truth and become who you already really are?

STEP FIVE: BE THE LIGHT

• Just be with the light. Just *be* the light. In the last chapter, I asked you to imagine a couple that had been together for many years sitting together quietly. Revisit that same ease and silence, and now sit with and be the light. Let that experience be what it is without thinking about or manipulating it, without searching for any answers, and without wanting anything from it. You'll find that, by simply being the light, the light takes over and invites you into itself in whatever way is important. In this sense, it's not necessary to know or understand all that the light is doing.

On January 11, 1992, the Sixth Sun rose, the color of the sunlight changed, the vibration of the sunlight became faster and gentler, and we began metabolizing a different quality of energy. It is difficult to test this new light energy in a laboratory because, through science, we do not yet understand light as a living being … but in time we will prove that it is a living biological being with intelligence and the source of our own intelligence.

DON MIGUEL RUIZ [37]

THE INSPIRATIONAL PERSPECTIVE

• My inner light sparkles with all the joy and magic of the stars.

• I live in an amazing world. Everything I see is brightly lit by divine light.

• My pulsating emotions and impulse-fired brain resonate with my divine light.

• Divine light shows me my true nature. Through the eyes of light, I am perfect.

- I am the light of God in motion. I am living in and spreading light everywhere.

- Everyone and everything I see is made of light. What a wonderful way to live!

- God's light is my light. With God sparkling within me, I can achieve anything.

- I am light! With light as my connector, I am one with everything in the universe!

- Divine light is a powerful tool. I now use it to heal and transform any situation.

- With the dazzling tool of light, I can and will overcome any and all obstacles.

- I am filled with the light of life. Every cell in my body reflects this awesome light.

- The light in my heart illuminates everything that I see. Life looks so beautiful.

- The light of God shines in and through everything in my daily experience.

- With light as my mentor, I know that I am free, loved, powerful and perfect.

I am part of the whole, all of which is governed by nature. I am intimately related to all the parts, which are of the same kind as myself.

If I remember these two things, I cannot be discontented with anything that arises out of the whole, because I am connected with the whole.

MARCUS AURELIUS [38]

The World of Energy  *3*

The Scriptural Perspective
From Light to Energy

Light looked upon the vast space filled only with itself and declared, "It's time to express myself anew." In that very moment, infinite light brought forth from its radiance an extraordinary new form, one that had been quietly concealed within its inner potential—a mighty new force that came to be called *energy.*

Instantly, light went into action. It shifted its quiet radiance into a richly pulsating movement and re-created its shining elegance into an active, dynamic vibration. Now charged with a reverberating resonance, it excitedly pulsated its way anew through space, generating rich waves of light-empowered energy. It magnified and expanded itself, and took on this new energetic form, now moving freely in a rhythmic, lively dance on the spacious dance floor of the universe.

Indeed, light was not only its own spacious and intangible radiance, it could now be felt—palpably sensed and experienced—as powerful, surging movement. Energy, freshly created, became a wondrously alive, vigorously moving, unashamedly vital presence everywhere.

Through its limitless pulsating, vibrating and generating qualities, energy created and re-created itself many times over, appearing as a multitude of innovative forms. Indeed, energy's most outstanding, impressive quality was its capacity to create the tangible from the intangible, the visible from the invisible, the material from the etheric. In fact, from that moment on, it did so with force and power, wonder and magnificence, passion and commitment. Light had impressively created itself anew in an amazing and impressive way.

Thus, the creative energy of the stars brought forth meteors, asteroids and planets, and on certain planets new phenomena of energy-propelled life emerged. On the planet called earth, the unique vibration of its

In the beginning there was endless space in which nothing existed but Tawa, the sun spirit, who gathered the elements of space and added some of his own substance, thereby creating the First World.

Spider Grandmother (came), to lead them on a long journey during which they changed form and grew. ...

By the time they arrived in the Third World, they had become people. Then, led by Spider Grandmother and her twin sons, the people climbed up ... into the upper world, the present Fourth World of the Hopis.

HOPI CREATION STORY[1]

The energy of life flows from the uncreated emptiness out into the planes of manifestation.

As the energy of life comes into manifestation, it becomes more visible.

At first it takes form as a pattern of energy, a fluid, dynamically flowing reality out of which the primal oneness of creation begins to differentiate itself.

Finally the energy of creation enters the physical plane and becomes a part of the world of the senses, at which time it becomes fixed into matter, into a physical form or event.

LLEWELLYN VAUGHN-LEE [2]

light gave birth to a magnetically charged, richly creative energy that had never before existed—an energy called *love*. Quickly, love became earth's dominant energy resource, its dynamic and creative power, the prevailing presence on the planet that now housed limitless potential for energy-rich life.

Love instantly became a vigorous and powerful energetic force—in fact, the central creative power on earth—and swiftly went into lively action. Amplifying the universe's endless light, love's creative power gave birth to innumerable embodiments of life, causing them to appear and disappear over billions of years. Countless offspring—rocks, oceans, plants, animals—were brought forth from the wondrous marriage of earth's creativity and love.

Single-celled creatures materialized, divided and multiplied into complex organisms. Over great spans of time, these life forms joined together to develop remarkable aptitudes and ever-greater levels of intricacy. More and more, all life became capable of feeling and experiencing the very enlivening energies that created it.

After eons, earth's love-powered energy conceived and brought forth human offspring, distinctive creatures with a heightened capacity for self-awareness. Slowly, these beings began to experience themselves not just as universal beings of light, but as strongly feeling, sentient, conscious beings—*human* beings made up of dynamic, moving, creative energy.

Yes, in humanity, the light had produced a life form with miraculous possibilities: the ability to sense, experience and enjoy its every fantastic creation. Gradually, human beings evolved to experience the multiple, truly limitless expressions of love, energy and creativity that filled the planet's endearing space. Their capacity for enjoying feelings, emotions and energies became markedly alive and finely tuned. They came to celebrate and take pleasure in the many tantalizing expressions of this wondrous world of energy—sexually, physically, musically, emotionally, mentally and spiritually.

Light, in creating itself anew as vibrant energy and creative love, had indeed brought about an entire world of fresh possibilities for joy and fulfillment. Some came to call this new world the Garden of Eden.

Materially, human beings could now experience the earth as their mother and the sun as their father. Spiritually, they felt earth's light-filled love as their mother and divine essence as their father.

Best of all, the human family could now rediscover and celebrate itself as an embodiment of earth's love-filled energy, as an expression of the universe's radiant light, and as a creation of the pure essence of God.

THE MYTHICAL PERSPECTIVE
From Light to Energy

A number of years ago, I made up an amusing story about how you and I first moved from a space of universal light to being creatures of earthly energy. I've since labeled this creative fable "The Cosmic Travel Agent." I hope you find it both entertaining and insightful. It goes like this.

There you were, hanging out in the far reaches of the universe, living as a radiant beam of light. Your whole nature was light and, as such, you simply floated around the universe, enjoying yourself, celebrating the infinite and unending space, and having an all-round good time—as light. Then, one day, you bumped into another being of light, a friend of yours who also, coincidentally, happened to be your cosmic travel agent.

After you exchanged greetings, your travel agent asked, "How are you doing?"

You answered, "Well, I'm doing just fine. Everything's really great, and I love the life of a light being. But you know, strange as it may seem, I'm starting to want a change of scenery. Being a light being is great, of course, but I'm beginning to long for a different kind of experience, something a bit more exciting. Have any suggestions?"

Your cosmic travel agent's beam lit up, and he responded excitedly, "Oh, have I got just the place for you! Way over in the far reaches of the universe, there's this adorable galaxy called the Milky Way. Well, in a small, out-of-the-way section of that galaxy, a group of planets revolve around this small star called the sun, and one of the planets is called earth."

He continued, "You wouldn't believe what they've got going over in that part of the universe. Look at us. We're just these light beams, gliding around, having a nice time. All we ever know and experience is endless, wondrous light. That's really awesome, of course, but guess what they have on earth—they have energy!"

Mystified, you ask, "Energy? What's that?"

Love the moment, and the energy of that moment will spread beyond all boundaries.

CORITA KENT [3]

Your cosmic travel agent fills you in. "Well I had no idea what it was either, but trust me. I've sent a few people over there, and the reports I've gotten back are flabbergasting. First of all, with energy, they say they can feel. So they can not only *be* light and enjoy it, they can also *feel* light in lots of different ways."

You wonder out loud, "Feel light in different ways? I don't understand."

Your agent tries to explain. "Well, first, get this—they have energy-filled bodies."

"Bodies!" you exclaim. "What in heaven's name are those?"

"It's hard to describe, but bodies are what show up when light becomes energy and energy expresses itself in a form that you can actually touch and see. Bodies can do all sorts of things." The travel agent goes on, "Human bodies can feel things. For example, they have sensors that allow them to experience tastes and hear what they call sounds. They can touch and feel anything—different textures, even the earth itself. They have eyes that can see light as though it were matter, and even see it in different colors.

"These people can also feel emotions. They can feel happy and sad, loving and hateful, powerful and afraid. Can you imagine such a thing—being able to experience a full range of feelings?"

Obviously, your friend's description of earth is a lot more than you can grasp right away. However, like any great salesbeing, the agent enthusiastically offers even more details about this phenomenon called energy. "Then, they have this sexual capacity where they can connect their bodies together and feel the energy of love in physical ways that you and I can't even begin to understand."

The cosmic travel agent now moves on to describe earth's other energies—love and power, for example—and how these dynamic forces give birth to all sorts of other forms. Then, he concludes by saying, "The whole purpose of life on earth seems to be to experience God's essence not just as light, as we do, but as countless experiences of energy-filled forms."

You're stunned ... and remarkably, mysteriously impressed. At this point, you watch these words exude from your personal light source, "Wow! This is amazing! I've never heard of anything like that." You conclude with a roaring, "Sign me up!"

Your travel agent does indeed sign you up, and poof! There you are. You wake up as a newborn infant on earth, and, sure enough, you have

Knowledge was inherent in all things.

The world was a library and its books were the stones, leaves, grass, brooks, and the birds and animals that shared, alike with us, the storms and blessings of earth.

We learned to do what only the student of nature ever learns, and that was to feel beauty.

This appreciation enriched Lakota existence. Life was vivid, pulsing; nothing was casual and commonplace.

The Indian lived—lived in every sense of the word—from his first to his last breath.

CHIEF LUTHER STANDING BEAR[4]

eyes through which you can see colors, shapes and moving things. You can see light as you've never seen it before—tangibly. You hear people "oohing" and "ahhing" over you. They're clearly happy and excited to have you around. Then you notice that you can feel the air on your tender skin. When people touch, hug and kiss you, you experience a sensation that's just wonderful. Soon they cover you with deliciously soft blankets in your crib.

After you've grown a little, you start to crawl on the rug and in the grass. You smell the fragrant plants, feel the cool earth, and watch the leaves dance in the wind. You think, "I never dreamed that light could make itself into energy, let alone that it could feel so good. None of my light-being friends out there would believe me if I told them that light could become such a powerful, energetic force, and that energy could take the form of all these things that I can taste, touch, see, feel, hear, explore and play with. What a great planet to be on! What a wondrous universe to live in! I love energy!"

THE HUMAN PERSPECTIVE
From Light to Energy

What an astonishing phenomenon our human world of energy is! And yet most of us tend to take our energetic make-up for granted. After all, it has been our primary means of experience and style of activity since our human race came into existence—it's simply what we have come to know. So, it's easy for us to miss the extraordinary beauty, wonder and power that living in this energy-rich world affords us. Come with me then; let's re-explore our energy-alive world with a fresh willingness to rediscover our inherent state of awe.

Energy, as we know, is a vital and moving force—in fact, it's the basic *life* force that creates and re-creates us humanly every day. It's that pulsing, vibrant, lively resonance that animates and supports everything in and around us, everything that we can see and sense. Indeed, behind the scenes, energy generates our thinking, infuses life into our bodies, and supports literally everything we do.

Yes, energy takes our light nature and, by creating it into noticeable and workable forms, makes our life more graspable, tangible and enjoyable. Through energy we can actually *feel* everything in and around us—our divine roots in our core, our intimate connectedness to everything around us, and our feelings of love, to name just a few.

Your lives are tapestries of such great beauty. The threads move together in endless patterns and colors both vivid and subtle. The warp extends from the apex of heaven to the core of the earth mother; the woof winds in and out, weaving all the wondrous possibilities of creation into life's fabric. Above, below, all around: they are all one cloth. Wrap yourself in beauty.

CYNTHIA LANE[5]

Energy underlies all life, flows in certain patterns, along specific paths, affecting and connecting matter and consciousness alike.

LLEWELLYN VAUGHN-LEE[6]

Matter—the kind of 'stuff' that is made up of particles joined in nuclei joined in atoms joined in molecules … —is not a distinct reality. It is energy bound in quantized wave-packets.

ERVIN LASZLO[7]

Without energy, we are purely and simply light beings; with energy we are light beings with pizzazz.

POWER AND LOVE

That pizzazz definitely deserves a closer look. Many years ago, it occurred to me that when divine essence sparked itself gloriously into radiant manifestation, it took on three remarkable, miraculous forms. The first form, as we know, is *light*—that luminous and brilliant expression of the divine that is so preciously inherent in our deepest nature. Then, as light reinvented itself ingeniously into energy-charged pulsations, two other divine expressions burst onto the feel-able stage of life—*power* and *love.*

Wondrously, here on earth, we can connect with our own cosmic roots and divine source not just as essence, but in three innovative and exceptional ways: as infinite light, creative power and enriching love. It's our privilege to view everything in life through the experiential lenses of these three remarkable phenomena.

In fact, if we interpret the Hebrew biblical description of our human nature—that we are indeed created "in the image and likeness of God"—in accordance with the Christian description of God as a vibrant trinity, we stumble upon an amazing discovery. We find ourselves created in the image and likeness of a God who is Father—creative *power,* Son—infinite *love,* and Spirit—radiant *light.* This marvelous coincidence implies, of course, that you and I are, at our core, creatively powerful, completely love-filled and dynamically light-inspired. Indeed, we hold these three dynamic qualities in our very nature—both for our personal fulfillment and as creative tools in building our lives. Now that's a life worth showing up to!

We've explored light in our last chapter and are clear that light gives us dynamic life and inspires us vibrantly every day. Let's look more deeply into the next two aspects of our created nature: our creative power and our exquisite love.

OUR CREATIVE POWER

Because our light nature has beamed itself miraculously into the remarkable form of energy—and because you and I actually *are* that energy—we literally share in the dynamic creative *power* of God. Yes, the very power that sparked pure essence into radiant light, the authority that produced the amazing light show that emerged from the Big

Bang, the same force that daily produces every creation imaginable is wondrously present here and now, in this three-dimensional space that holds and sustains you and me. That initial dynamic power of creation is literally ours to enjoy and use—in the form of our very own creative energy.

This dynamic, energetic power is so inherent in our created nature, so intimate a part of who we are, that our every thought instantly activates our natural drive to create, our innate urge to take charge, and our inborn desire to make something happen. Power, accompanied by its intrinsic impulse to create, is present in our every focus, active in our body's every subatomic motion, and soaring through our every experience.

To share in the ongoing divine creation of life ... to be an active participant in the potent spark that daily ignites new life and brings forth new expressions ... to be an actual co-creator with God in establishing our world—these are compelling reasons to claim our aliveness, to embrace the fullness of our humanity, and to live in awe of this planet's magnetic charm!

Every day we call forth our resident power and go about creating our lives with this commanding tool in hand. We make meaningful plans; we create cherished relationships; we take charge of whatever personal challenges arrive on our plate. We use this magical power to heal our bodies' infirmities, to transform our emotional pain, and to propel ourselves into entirely new stages of life. With our personal power as our intimate tool, we develop a deeper sense of confidence, enhance our belief in ourselves, and call ourselves to stand more firmly in our authority.

It's no doubt then that being human brings us into a totally new relationship with the divine—indeed, with all life everywhere—because we share in life's awesome power to create. While living only in essence or as a being of light is wonderful and awe-inspiring, I think we must admit that being in our energy-powered human form is tangibly more interesting, engaging and compelling.

No matter how much we may have taken our creative power for granted or focused on its daunting, sometimes intimidating challenges, it's simply true that life here on earth was masterfully designed with remarkable magical possibilities and inventive potential. And you and I are right in the middle of this innovative show of wonder—because we

Simple physics tells us that energy and information leave the body and go out into space. It reaches our loved ones and our pets and plants, it extends to the sky, and yes, logically, the electromagnetic fields expand into the 'vacuum' of space at the speed of light, 186,000 miles per second.

GARY E. R. SCHWARTZ
AND LINDA G. S. RUSSEK [10]

Joy is the dynamic aspect of Being. When the creative power of the universe becomes conscious of itself, it manifests as joy.

ECKHART TOLLE [11]

share in life's gift of power. Yes, we're light beings with the pizzazz of creative power ...

OUR ENRICHING LOVE

... and with the pizzazz of unending love. Yes, because of light's tantalizing gift of pulsating energy, we as human beings have an astonishing, unique heritage—to experience the lighted-ness of life as *love* ... to feel the daily embrace of love's pulsating, fulfilling and renewing energy. We know the magic of loving and being loved.

Love permeates every aspect of our daily lives—it's alive in our songs and present in all our relationships. It influences our thoughts, feelings and interactions. In truth, love is the most fundamental, primal force in our lives. It guides us in all our decisions (with all respect to the supposedly central role of logic!) and directs us in every action.

There's no way to escape love's profound presence in our lives. Because of love, you and I can bond deeply, connect tenderly with life, and experience a vital oneness with our creative source. As loving persons, we can know the warmth of a gentle touch, feel true compassion in a warm-hearted moment, and experience the inner glow of intimate connection. Indeed, love will have its way—we can neither suppress nor deny its active and creative richness. Love is who we are, from start to finish.

As I envision it, we all are born in light's loving embrace ... raised in the midst of life's swirling energies of love ... and at special moments initiated into love's vaster realms of possibilities. Further, love holds us daily in its protective embrace ... inspires us again and again with its alluring magnetism ... and even heals our personal pain with its invisible, caring touch.

Love is, without a doubt, our most endearing inner resource. When we love ourselves and those around us, we not only see life through the compelling filter of love, we actually create our lives to look more and more like love. When we are actively loving in every aspect of our lives, we draw to ourselves both persons and situations that invite love to move to the fore and initiate us anew into itself even more richly.

What would we be without love? Certainly, we would be innately logical, like the illustrious Mr. Spock, viewing our lives as full of level-headed possibilities. Also, we would be aware of our creative power, accomplishing our objectives with success but with little sense of satisfaction or joy in those accomplishments. We would approach

Love is like infinity: You can't have more or less infinity ... Infinity just is, and that's the way I think love is, too.

MISTER (FRED) ROGERS [12]

To love yourself is to love and thank all of existence.

MASARU EMOTO [13]

Such love does the sky now pour, that whenever I stand in a field, I have to wring out the light When I get home.

ST. FRANCIS OF ASSISI [14]

Real love is a love that opens itself to all possibilities and is not caught in the patterns of limitation. It carries the song of freedom ... and those who have given themselves to love ... know the secret places where love manifests.

LLEWELLYN VAUGHN-LEE [15]

our relationships as practical and helpful, but with little sense of deep connection, no delight from the intimate bond, and only the barest experience of oneness. In short, without love we'd feel quite empty, alone and lifeless.

So often we contrast love with its seeming opposites—anger, fear or hurt, to name a few. In fact, we sometimes feel so locked in our hurtful emotions that we can't access a feeling of love at all. We feel that we've lost love's gifts and are left swirling in the pit of our personal pain.

In truth, our painful feelings are not in any way love's opposites; they are actually the very experience of love itself, filtered through our current emotional pain. Yes, anger—and depression, fear and so many other pain-based emotions—are the best version of real love that we are capable of in the moment. It's just that our emotional needs for safety bring love into our experience not in its embracing and endearing form, but in mutated forms, like fear, hurt or anger.

Yes, these emotionally painful feelings are still the real thing—love itself—albeit wrapped in the self-defensive package of protection and languaged with a bravado that may sound quite convincing in the short term. Even though we may be certain that we are not loving or loved in that moment, we are in truth totally filled with love—in the best way we know how to feel it. Indeed, love is everywhere; it's inescapable; it's us.

Let's look at love through our divine roots. Have you noticed how often we refer to God as love? We frequently hear the phrase, "God is Love!" We look at Jesus, Buddha and other powerful spiritual teachers as personifying God's grace-filled love. Many view the current Dalai Lama as the embodiment of the Buddha of Love and Compassion. Yes, whenever we experience our personal or human roots—our existential origins and cosmological beginnings—we can't escape a renewed discovery of our creative source, loving us vibrantly into being.

Indeed, God, our essential source and infuser of light, is love. In fact, on this feeling-based, passionate planet, love may be the most tangible way in which we can experience the divine. Especially if we feel cut off from our divine source, as most of us do, how comforting it is to have love's concrete way of relating to that beautiful source!

In God, we have a protective father figure, a loving mother, a devoted caretaker and protector, a grace-filled provider of our needs, an unconditionally loving forgiver of our seeming faults, and a generous embracer of everything that we are. We can feel an intimate connection

I think it's essential to love yourself, to be able to thank yourself, and to respect yourself. When you do so, each of these vibrations will be sent out into the cosmos, and the great symphony of that harmonic vibration will enfold our planet with waves, such as those that cherish your heaven-granted life.

MASARU EMOTO [16]

One word frees us of all the weight and pain of life: That word is love.

SOPHOCLES [17]

Jesus uses this word [the Aramaic word rahme] (usually translated as 'love') to express that the highest form of love gives birth to a new sense of self, in both ourselves and others. We can help those we love become who they are really meant to be.

NEIL DOUGLAS-KLOTZ [18]

and powerful bond with an infinite source that would otherwise be unfathomable. We can pray passionately and talk intimately to this all-knowing one who loves us. We can even feel the very essence of this creative source in ourselves. How blessed we are, because of the mighty presence of love!

THE AWESOME WORLD OF FEELINGS

Love doesn't stop there. It introduces us to the exquisite world of *feeling* and *sensing*. We can not only know and understand our life and its circumstances, the grand perspectives of the mind, but we can also experience them as sensations, emotions and energies, perspectives of the body, heart and spirit. We can literally sense life's pulsations as our own vibrations and feel its magical flows moving in and through us. It's been said, "To feel life is to know life."

Let's look at three specific expressions of love-rich energy that touch us daily: our sexuality, emotionality and physicality.

- Sexuality

What a privilege we have—to experience an intimate connection with our own *sexuality* and the sexuality of others ... to feel the sensual affinity that we have with other people ... and to share in the very sexual energy of our own love-charged planet!

Sexuality—electrically charged, emotionally stimulating, filled with primal passion and infinite pleasure—is one of our world's most gratifying feelings. Just think, if light had remained light and not created itself anew into energy, we would never experience the privilege of earth's tantalizing sexual delights.

Most of us live in societies with ambivalent and conflicted attitudes about sexuality. We feel exhilarated by and grateful for our experience of sexuality, and guilty about it at the same time. As we know, this basic, primal aspect of our human experience has come to be associated over recent millennia with feelings of shame, guilt and sin. While a sense of shame and unworthiness is indeed deeply ingrained in our human psyche—a factor that we shall look at in some detail in our next chapter—in truth, there is no objective or spiritually grounded reason to localize that sense of guilt in the realm of our sexuality.

Rather, our sexuality is as natural, beautiful and sacred as anything else on our precious planet. In fact, like all feelings, sexuality stems from the very divine source that is infused in every aspect of life.

With

passion pray.
With passion work.
With passion make love.
With passion eat and drink
and dance and play.
Why look like a dead fish
in this ocean
of God?

RUMI [19]

I want to live for ecstasy. Small doses, moderate loves, all half-shades, leave me cold. I like extravagance ... books which overflow from their covers, sexuality which bursts the thermometers.

ANAÏS NIN [20]

When we experience moments of ecstasy—in play, in stillness, in art, in sex—they come not as an exception, an accident, but as a taste of what life is meant to be. ... Ecstasy ... can be the expectation of every day.

GABRIELLE ROTH [21]

It's our human way of sharing in the divine act of creation, of living experientially in God's dynamic generative quality, and of experiencing, briefly or in every moment, the unending ecstasy of divine love.

Every aspect of life here on earth is sexual. The planet's underlying sexual rhythms are sweetly alive in our every connection with nature, powerfully present in our conversations with our friends, and lovingly soaring—sometimes gently, sometimes richly—through our bodies and emotions, every day of our lives. While we typically associate sexuality with the act of intercourse, it is a much more vast, all-encompassing and wondrous experience of life, one that never leaves our energetic fabric, one that keeps love beautifully alive within us every second.

- Emotions

Consider also our emotions. Where else in this universe of possibilities can we experience the *feeling* aspects of life as we do here on planet earth? Feelings, emotions, sensations ... joy, excitement, happiness ... sadness, fear, anger ... love, pain, intimacy ... peacefulness, agitation, restlessness—these are only a few of the thousands of feelings that flood our bodies, flow through our nervous systems, and permeate our emotional system.

Imagine what life would be like without feeling. We would not experience the joy of a brilliant sunrise, the warmth of sunshine on our skin, or the romantic feeling of witnessing the moon on a starlit night. We'd miss the fulfillment of being in love, the wonder of imaginative play, and the feeling of empowerment that comes from dealing effectively with life's challenges. Yes, life without feelings would be, in short, dull and dreary! How appropriate, indeed how perfect it is to enjoy and celebrate life in and through our emotional feelings!

Yet, as with sexuality, we often get lost in our learned value judgments about our emotions. Most of us view different emotions as either desirable or undesirable, healthy or unhealthy, good or bad. These dualistic evaluations can easily lead us to distrust certain emotions, especially those that we've decided are "negative," and to avoid or actually run from some of our deepest, most important feelings.

Could it be—and I strongly believe it is!—that such value judgments are arbitrarily invented by us, are based on a very narrow perspective, and have no basis in any bigger truth? From the perspective of light, where we perceive our precious emotions through the eyes of unity rather than duality, we don't even have a concept of right and wrong,

Infinite riches are all around you if you will open your mental eyes and behold the treasure house of infinity within you. There is a gold mine within you from which you can extract everything you need to live life gloriously, joyously, and abundantly.

JOSEPH MURPHY [22]

My Time on this Earth has been but a blink of an eye. I thank God for allowing me the Time to love, smile, cry and hopefully touch a few precious souls.

RAIN BEAR [23]

Life is so generous a giver, but we, judging its gifts by their covering, cast them away as ugly or heavy or hard. Remove the covering and you will find beneath it a living splendor, woven in love by wisdom, with power. Welcome it, grasp it, and you touch the angel's hand that brought it to you.

FRA ANGELICO [24]

Those times when we're grounded in our body, pure in our heart, clear in our mind, rooted in our soul, and suffused with the energy, the spirit of life, are our birthright.

GABRIELLE ROTH [25]

What if today were your very first day here on earth? See your body as if it were new. Yes, you have been born in a big way, fully grown, with the size and age perfect for an earth experience. Nice job!

ROSE ROSETREE [26]

good or bad. We see only the beauty and importance of "what is"—the essence and core truth of our feelings.

And so, emotions simply "are"—none of them essentially right or wrong. They move within us and express through us with great value and worth. They are expressions of authentic feelings, voices of underlying truth, echoes of deeply felt convictions. Indeed, they all deserve to be listened to, heard and entertained—with respect, honor and esteem.

Also, our subconscious mind never judges or condemns our emotional feelings. While the conscious mind searches for moral evaluation, our subconscious wisdom looks only for the deeper meaning or symbolism of our emotions, always asking, "What is their significance? What are they trying to express?" Our subconscious self embraces each emotion as valuable, meaningful and important.

Subconsciously, our emotions have permission to breathe, express and be fully themselves. What wisdom lives in our subconscious depths! What great expressions of life and self are our glorious emotions!

I deeply believe that our human emotions are among the greatest energetic gifts that we have the privilege to experience here on earth. Though it is already completely natural and inherent in our human make-up, we often forget how to receive those gifts. If we can re-learn to embrace them, listen to their wisdom, and align with their unique style of speaking our deeper truth, we will have leapt powerfully into another way of celebrating the love-filled life that surrounds us.

• Physicality

Our *bodies*—those seemingly material forms that serve as the support system for our human feelings—are equally marvelous. Ah, the wonder of having and experiencing a human body! Even though they are, as we might recall, 99.9 percent light, we have the special privilege here on earth of experiencing our light bodies in so many tangible, physical, organic ways.

Recall the joy of savoring a delicious meal or the pleasure of a great sleep. Remember the beautiful feeling that comes from being touched by someone, the exhilaration that follows a vigorous exercise, or the thrill you experience when you overcome a dangerous situation. Notice how your body reacts and feels when you view the beauty of another person's body, how your heart pounds as you watch an exciting sports event, or how your physical sensations swoon with excitement as you watch an elegantly danced ballet.

As we can see, these bodies of ours are incredible, magnificent vehicles for wonderful personal experience and heightened human fulfillment. How ingenious of essence—to create itself into light … then to fashion light into energy … and finally to mold energy into physical matter! How fortunate we are to have this energy-filled playground on which to experience, enjoy and celebrate our magnificent bodies! It just could be that our cosmic travel agent was giving us a great tip when he invited us to this dream vacation here on earth!

With these fresh perspectives, it is an easy step for us to proclaim: This dynamic world of intimate sexuality, emotional feelings and bodily physicality is an utterly divine experience … an infinite blessing of loving grace … and an unfathomable manifestation of God's inventive creativity! Being human, when we examine it in its purely divine design, is an utterly captivating experience of the miracle of life. It's our essence in creative action, our light in radiant expression, and our energy in delicious manifestation. How blessed we are!

LIFE'S PURPOSE—TO EXPLORE AND PLAY IN ENERGY

Imagine this: the main reason that you and I came to this planet is to experience infinite life—its pure essence, expansive light and endless creativity—in thousands of energy-rich, energy-alive and energy-filled ways.

Notice the fulfillment that we feel in experiencing our bodies and emotions, creating intimate friendships, discovering new ideas and perspectives, and exploring our sexual and sensual feelings. Recall how meaningful it is to appreciate a moving work of art, experience an inspired moment, and create satisfying achievements.

We can easily assert that life on this precious planet is all about having experiences—feeling ones, intimate ones, entrepreneurial ones, and so many others. By exploring and playing in the awesome world of energy, we are connected to the life force and vitality of everything and everyone around us.

In fact, if we look at our lives starting from birth, we notice that exploring and playing in energy is exactly what we've been doing all along. No matter what other preoccupations have captured our attention, it is energy that moves all around us, flows dynamically through us, and connects us intimately to the whole world. With energy as our vital life force, we are indeed one with everything.

The power to live a full, adult, living, breathing life in close contact with what I love—the earth and the wonders thereof, the sea, the sun … I want to enter into it, to be a part of it, to live in it, to learn from it … I want to be all that I am capable of becoming.

KATHERINE MANSFIELD [27]

In this my green world
Flowers birds are hands
They hold me
I am loved all day
All this pleases me
I am amused
I have to laugh from crying
Trees mountains are arms
I am loved all day

KENNETH PATCHEN [28]

*We have reached a point in our
evolution that requires us to speak
'energy' fluently.*

CAROLINE MYSS [29]

*I thank you God for most this
amazing day: for the leaping
greenly spirits of trees
and a blue true dream of sky;
and for everything which is
… infinite, which is yes
how should tasting touching
hearing seeing breathing
any … human merely being
doubt unimaginable You?*

E.E. CUMMINGS [30]

*To see a World in a Grain
of Sand
And a Heaven in a Wild Flower,
Hold Infinity in the palm of
your hand
And Eternity in an hour.*

WILLIAM BLAKE [31]

The truth is, we came here precisely for this stimulating, energy-filled experience of the infinite. No matter how much we may have numbed ourselves to our feelings or disconnected ourselves from our body's energy-expressing wisdom, our divinely-rooted energetic nature continues to call us daily to remember … and reconnect … and enjoy!

How often do you consciously appreciate the special gifts of sensing and feeling? Or close your eyes and simply let yourself be present to the way the wind feels on your skin? How frequently do you breathe in the refreshing fragrance of the air and notice how it makes you feel? Or fully appreciate the first bite of a fresh-picked apple or the taste of food that has been lovingly prepared? How regularly do you watch the sun set and the full moon rise and let them fill you with awe?

These phenomena are precious expressions of essence, spoken through the language of light and energy. The good news is this: we have the privilege of knowing life intimately, every day. We can clearly experience our divine source, tangibly and sensually, in every moment.

Why is this earth of ours so gift-wrapped with energy? Perhaps exactly for this singular purpose—to give us the honor of experiencing the absolute infinity of life in tangible, feel-able, fulfilling ways, and, in that daily celebration, to discover God anew, rejoice fully in life, and find the amazing wonder of existence!

Bernadette's Story

Stories, whether we hear or tell them, often hold clues to a subtle or hidden wisdom. In our modern movie-oriented times, films often play the role of storyteller for us. As such, if it's the right moment in our lives, we sometimes find an important message for us in a special movie.

A friend of a friend—I'll call her Bernadette—recently told me about just such an experience. As she watched a film made several years ago, called *City of Angels,* she gained a new level of clarity about the amazing privilege of approaching the divine through feeling—an extremely significant event for her at that time.

As Bernadette described it, the movie's central figure is an angel, "on duty" in Los Angeles. As in the earlier story of our cosmic traveler, the angel chooses to give up his celestial existence in order to be able to *feel*—in this case, love—in a richly human, emotional and physical way. His intimate time with his beloved human partner turns out to be unpredictably brief, but he chooses to remain irrevocably human, and to open to the wonders and challenges of human experience in other ways.

In the film's final scene, on a Los Angeles beach, the now-human angel is reminded of the celestial quality of existence that he has given up as he watches his angelic brethren perform a sacred sunrise ceremony in which he once participated. However, he is also keenly aware of the energy-rich gifts that he now possesses, gifts that the other angels cannot know. It's clear that they are unable to smell the sea or feel its revitalizing touch as he does, nor can they see the breathtaking colors of the dawn to which they pay homage.

The angels, in turn, recognize their former brother and watch him with curiosity and longing as he dives resolutely into the ocean waves, exploring, playing with and rejoicing in the ocean's power and in the magical, energized realm of feeling that is now his life.

From Bernadette's perspective, the angel-turned-human transcended his losses by embracing the genuinely divine possibilities entwined in the human capacity for feeling. She saw that each of us can celebrate all the possibilities that energy provides—love, power, movement, emotion, sexuality, beauty and more. She got the message that every experience and form, every expression of energy, is a special and wonder-filled path to our divine light and source. Experienced to its depths, energy lets us find heaven on earth—divine light and essence shining through every form.

OUR HUMAN POSSIBILITY ... OUR HUMAN CALLING

You and I have that very same capacity to find and celebrate our own divine nature in earth's energetic fabric. Let's remember, just as our essence reflects and embodies God's essence, so our human energy expresses that same divine nature. Wouldn't it be wonderful if we felt and perceived ourselves as the living embodiment of God's innate desire to create?

How endlessly satisfying it would be to feel ourselves as an intimate part of a divine creative act! After all, in our inventive depths lies an energy-charged generator of instincts and orientations—the original power and love of God—with which we can create our own world.

Imagine a life in which we are always aware of the joy of being a feeling, sensing, loving, empowered, dynamic, wonder-filled expression of the divine ... a life in which we experience our energetic aliveness every day, from our body's beating heart right down to the inspiring movement of our soul ... a richness of self resulting simply from our

The Great Spirit is heard in the twittering of birds, the rippling of the mighty waters, and the sweet breathing of the flowers.

ZITKALA-SA [32]

On a day when the wind is perfect the sail just needs to open and the world is full of beauty. Today is such a day.

RUMI [33]

In Native American culture, we see everything as being alive. Each living thing has a specific role as a teacher and family member. Everything on Earth, whether stone, tree, creature, cloud, sun, moon, or human being is one of our relatives ... they represent the sacred living extensions of the Great Mystery, placed here to help humankind evolve spiritually.

JAMIE SAMS [34]

Can you hear the heart of the Mother? It's beating.

Can you hear the songs of the wind? It's blowing.

Can you see the rays of the sun? It's shining.

Can you feel the cool water? It's flowing.

If you can experience these wonderful things, then you are truly experiencing Life.

RAIN BEAR [35]

It's really not that hard to stop and luxuriate in the joy and wonder of being. Children do it all the time. It's a natural human gift that should be at the heart of all our lives.

GABRIELLE ROTH [36]

China tea, the scent of hyacinths, wood fires and bowls of violets— that is my mental picture of an agreeable February afternoon.

CONSTANCE SPRY [37]

energetic connection with the whole world! This is already our daily fare—and can be more so if only we choose to notice and claim it.

Imagine what it would be like to be totally energized, overflowing with the vitality and fullness of our energy-rich make-up ... to embrace our personal energy—and that of everything and everyone around us—with complete trust in its perfection and capacity to lead us to the fulfillment of our earthly purpose. Imagine opening ourselves to all the divine gifts that are accessible to us in our energetic human form.

Thankfully, we have that opportunity. Simply because we have taken on a human form, we can experience God in a morning's sunrise, discover divine essence in the center of our souls, and celebrate the whole universe in a breath of air. We can find the poetry of life in an intimate relationship, uncover life's deeper mysteries in a brave embrace of our own emotions, and unearth nature's wonder while delighting in the night's light-studded stars.

We can feel the primal pleasures of life by exploring our sexuality, discover the wisdom of the divine by attuning sensitively to our own bodies, and learn the special language of light by embracing the miracle of a moment's inspiration. Indeed, we can find the blessings that lay hidden in our daily travels by showing up to the spaces between our words and opening ourselves to the eloquence of the bird's songs.

We are so energetically alive in our five senses, our human inventiveness, our colorful imagination, and our innate sense of awe. We participate in energy's—indeed, God's—riches when we feel the caress of love, the touch of closeness, and the joy of oneness. Certainly, we know the astonishing world of energy—and the absolute wonder of the divine—when we feel our personal power in our core, our truth's inspiration in our soul, and our creativity-generating motivation in our emotions.

Energy, in its myriad creative richness, fills every space in and around us, insatiably inviting us to new possibilities of living fully and abundantly. In each moment God literally speaks to us in and through this energetically alive world of personal experience. We can have it all, know it all and celebrate it all, simply by fully embracing, owning and participating in this wondrous world of energy. Shall we?

THE PERSONAL PERSPECTIVE
Embracing and being energy

The following five steps present a simple yet powerful method to help you move into the full vitality and divine wisdom of your energy. I offer them to you as an invitation to find your divine essence and radiant light in the unique language of your energy. I encourage you to walk through these five approaches in whatever ways your soulful depths inspire, moved by your profound light and propelled by your purest wisdom.

STEP ONE: ACKNOWLEDGE AND OWN YOUR ENERGY

- Acknowledge every form of energy that lives in you. For example, notice your sexual and sensual energies, primal energies, cellular and gut-level energies—and experience them as a real and natural part of you. Also focus on your love energies, creative energies, power energies and emotional energies. Acknowledge whatever energy comes to the forefront of your attention.

- Spend time with each of these energies as they appear in your awareness ... until each one starts to feel like a natural and familiar part of who you are. Own them all as dynamic, rich, organic aspects of your human nature.

- Open to feeling these energies as fully as you can, one by one. Let yourself sink into them, rather than thinking about them or trying to understand them from a distance. As you do, if any one evokes a sense of revulsion, pain, sadness, fear, anxiety or anger, invite yourself to a fresh acceptance of that energy within you. Do this in stages, if necessary. Be simple and direct. Remember that this emotion is just another expression of energy, and all energy is ultimately a sacred expression of God.

- Every emotion, whether comfortable or uncomfortable, happy or sad, has great value, meaning and purpose for that particular moment in your life. Open to each emotion that arises as completely as possible; feel it; accept it. Instead of fighting or denying it, make peace with it; acknowledge it; own it.

Deliverance is not for me in renunciation. I feel the embrace of freedom in a thousand bonds of delight. No, I will never shut the doors of my senses. The delights of sight and hearing and touch will bear thy delight. Yes, all my illusions will burn into illumination of joy, and all my desires ripen into fruits of love.

RABINDRANATH TAGORE [38]

STEP TWO: EMBRACE YOUR ENERGY

- Now that you have acknowledged and made peace with your energies, take the next step: embrace each one of them. Having accepted their presence, now take a step closer and invite yourself to a deep connection with them. Feel each energy, whatever it may be, as a useful, even valuable part of you, an important contribution to your life. Open yourself to a full relationship, even an intimacy, with every feeling, impulse and vibration that lives within you. Take your time. Really embrace those energies; feel close to them; touch them tenderly.

- Stay the course. Continually call yourself to make friends with your feelings, no matter what. Embracing your uncomfortable emotions may be difficult at first, especially if you have feared or avoided them. However, as many disciplines have recognized, "whatever you resist will persist." Therefore, step out of any resistance and start embracing your feelings. When you finally break down the barriers between yourself and whatever energy you've learned to fear, you will indeed find the profound truth, meaning and empowerment that lie hidden beneath its presence.

- Move gently and lovingly through this process. It may take time and repetition to complete itself. Don't feel discouraged if those long-hidden, carefully avoided feelings don't reveal themselves all at once. Love yourself through this part of the experience rather than pushing yourself.

- Remember that grace is your ally in all you attempt. Don't hesitate to ask for it. What might have been too difficult before could now prove easier than you imagine, as you become increasingly aware of the strength and immediacy of divine support. Ask for grace, and then take time to feel how that divine love pours through you and helps you soften and embrace even the most challenging emotions.

- Remember that your energy is innately sacred. In truth, every energy within and around you is a dynamic expression of your divine source, a beautiful expression of your God-self. Therefore, to be wary or distrustful of it is an expression of a limited interpretation and only creates pain. Say to yourself, "This energy (feeling, issue, pain, etc.) is my friend … is my friend … is my friend."

STEP THREE: ACCEPT YOUR ENERGY'S GIFTS
... AND CREATE WITH THEM

Your energy field—the vibrations of your body, the vitality of your emotions, the creativity of your chakras, and the radiance of your aura—offers you thousands of gifts daily. They give you grace-filled presents such as love, empowerment, creativity, joy, peace and a sense of wonder. They place feeling, movement, taste, sexuality, sight, hearing and touch at your disposal.

Many, many more gifts await you from within the wealth of your personal energy system. These might include the capacity to heal, the privilege of intimacy, the power to create abundance, and a feeling of fulfillment in every accomplishment. They might also involve your connection with your deepest self, your innermost knowing, the ability to feel other people's energies, the power to communicate and express yourself, the ability to forgive, and the skill to decide your own fate.

These are but a few of the innumerable gifts available to all of us. Thus:

- Invite yourself to receive your energy's gifts. Now that you have embraced and owned the many ways energy lives in you, let yourself explore and enjoy its countless possibilities. Even if you have taken these gifts for granted, they are the basis of life's meanings, purposes, fulfillment and joy. Invite yourself, therefore, to a fresh relationship with these offerings. Try saying these words, "I am open and receptive to whatever my energy gifts me with today."

- Now that you have invited yourself to receive these gifts, call on them throughout the day to support you in your activities. When you want to ignite your creativity, compassion and enthusiasm, for example, ask your energy to give you those exact gifts. If you feel a need to sharpen your awareness or empower your communication, reach into your energetic depths for power in these endeavors. When you discover that you need more trust or intimacy in your life, ask life's energy to support you in these arenas.

- Most especially, invite your energies to give you all their gifts with reckless abandon, with total dedication, and with deeply felt love. Rather than asking or praying for them timidly or half-heartedly—as we often do if we're feeling unworthy or shy—give yourself permission to reach out for them with gusto, confidence and authority. You deserve them, you know. You deserve them.

STEP FOUR: TAKE CHARGE OF YOUR ENERGY

- Once you start receiving more gifts from your energies—that is, once you become more aware of the many energetic presents that are regularly given to you every day—you're ready to take the next step. Here it is: in addition to being a grateful receiver of the wondrous gifts of the world of energy, take charge of your energies.

- Remind yourself that you are indeed a creator of energies. You're not just here on earth to experience the wonderful world of energetic creativity, you're also here to participate in the creative act itself. You're here to bring about fresh forms and expressions, with energy as your tool. Access your inner permission to be a co-creator with your energy. Just as energy is a healer, so also are you. Just as your love is a forgiving, embracing force, so also are you. You're the creator of your life.

- Now, totally united with your energies, call yourself to take charge. Become a fully alive, energetic player in every area of your life. Say to yourself, "I am master of my destiny … creator of my happiness … solver of my problems … inventor of my life." Say these words with dedicated, committed intention and heartfelt conviction.

- Now, calling upon your energy, if something in you needs healing, heal it. If a relationship needs loving attention, give yourself to it. If your life needs reinventing, make it happen—powerfully, creatively, lovingly and dynamically. Take a bold step into this creative role, refusing to back off or lose faith.

- Remind yourself that God designed you as a co-creative wielder of energetic power. Remember that it's your birthright to create your soul's truth into a real life form. Say to yourself, "I can do it. I am an energy-rich self, with an energy-filled nature and an energy-powered purpose. I claim my right to be that energy-propelled creator of my life right now."

STEP FIVE: BE ENERGY

- Be energy. Be the spirit that moves your energy. Be the power that drives your energy. Be the love that infuses life into your energy. In short, identify with and become the full, energy-based self that you are.

- Acknowledge that you are in truth the very energies that express in your attitude, mind, beliefs, assumptions, feelings, emotions and nature. Own that you are the total energy that lives so wondrously and beautifully in you.

By so doing, you will not only participate completely in this wondrous world of energy, but also become the masterful expresser of its unbounded possibilities.

Genius is mainly an affair of energy.

MATTHEW ARNOLD [39]

THE INSPIRATIONAL PERSPECTIVE

- Energy! What a gift! It makes my essence and light feel-able and real to me.

- I can now taste, see, feel, hear and smell God the world over. Thank you, God!

- My energy is sacred. Its every form is a beautiful expression of my source.

- With my precious energy, I experience and create endlessly with my light.

- I am the living embodiment and expression of God's desire to create.

- Creative power is my heritage. With every breath I create my life!

- I am blessed with so many emotions and sensations. How rich my life is!

- With energy as my friend, I now call forth a truly fulfilling life.

- My sexuality is my personalized version of the divine spark of creation.

- On this wonder-filled planet, I can experience God and love everywhere.

- Divine light speaks through my feelings. What a glorious way to know God!

- My energy is filled with life's splendor. What a blessing to host that splendor!

- In loving my body, I'm loving everything, even love. Thank you, body!

- I live on a love-filled planet. I can find and feel love everywhere I look.

- My emotions and energies enrich my experience. I embrace them all!

- I choose to create a magical life, so I now embrace life's magical energies.

- My body speaks divine wisdom. I choose to listen to its loving whisperings.

- I see God in the morning sunrise, in the bird's song, in my beautiful self.

- I love my emotions. They express the "me" that is wise, alive and vibrant.

- "The hills are alive with the sound of music!" So is all life … and so am I!

Imagine this
Among the infinite worlds and universes of life
A single solitary planet
Is reserved for dance
For the alive vibrant exciting
Pulsing sparkling dazzling
Refreshing delighting energizing
Dance of life

Who wouldn't come
To such an enticing planet
Once invited as an honored guest
To this passionate dance of life
Who wouldn't choose to attend
This fun gleeful crazy party
Just when your little inner voice told you
You could use a little fun

Welcome to the ball
Come in ... enjoy this outrageous planet
In its wild movement and compelling sway
Make yourself at home on the dance floor of touching emotion
Find pleasure in the intimate dance of heartful love
In the sensual tango of energetic passion
In the serene waltz of nature's elegance
In the moving rumba of primal intensity
In the inspiring ballet of life's beauty

How she moves and sways
Glitters and glows
Senses and feels
Breathes and blows
This planet of dancing swirling twirling ecstasy

How exquisite her body
Bending willingly to the sun's mighty touch
How inspiring her soul
Impressing its grace into her very winds
How delightful her spirit
Flowing lovingly through her animated senses

Let's surrender to her party's embrace
Let our hair down, way down
As the spirit of the dance takes us over
Let's find our soul's inviting movement
Open our body's rusty valves
Unleash our psyche's unbridled force
And let loose with our endless might

We've come to the dance
Yes, the dance of life
Ah the dance of life

BILL BAUMAN [40]

THE ARRIVAL OF AWARENESS

THE SCRIPTURAL PERSPECTIVE
From Energy to Awareness

In the beginning, pure essence sparked itself into a vast, luminous light. Light, in turn, morphed itself into a dynamic field of energy. Energy then wondrously generated love, its signature expression. Thus it was that love became the centerpiece of all creative activity in that universe containing the small planet called earth.

After eons of creativity, love expressed itself in a new way on this tiny planet. It manifested a fresh embodiment of life called human beings, and, even more impressively, placed within this unique species a special capacity——the ability to become aware, to be conscious. Yes, the divine source lovingly infused into the human brain the replica of its own awareness.

Human beings now possessed the capacity to know, the power to be aware of themselves and life, and the ability to join consciously with their own divine, creative nature.

Thus, humans began a gradual and remarkable evolution toward becoming conscious, mindful, thinking, intuitive, wisdom-oriented beings. Their new gift of *conscious awareness* was exceptional and unprecedented. It was generously given so members of the human family could develop and expand it, and with its awesome power, come to know themselves intimately and understand the mysterious workings of life.

Over many millennia, the human brain developed and the mind's cognitive abilities grew. This gifted species began to think deeply and imaginatively about the world around them. They developed beliefs about their origins, ideas about creation, and theories about the purpose of life.

God made the world as a garden in which He himself took delight. He made man and gave to man the task of sharing in His own divine care for created things. He let man decide for himself how created things were to be interpreted, understood and used ... Thus in his intelligence man, by the act of knowing, imitated something of the creative love of God for his creatures. While the love of God, looking upon things, brought them into being, the love of man, looking upon things, reproduced the divine idea, the divine truth, in man's own spirit.

THOMAS MERTON[1]

From himself (atmanah) he also drew forth the mind, which is both real and unreal, likewise from the mind egoism, which possesses the function of self-consciousness ... moreover, the soul ... and, in their order, the five organs which perceive the objects of sensation.

MANU SMRTI [2]

Life is a state of consciousness.

EMMET FOX [3]

Gradually, this fortunate species came to discover that their innovative gift was intended and available not just for their own knowing, but also for co-creating their human world. They remembered that the creative power of essence was a part of their own make-up. Thus, they began to use their ingenious thinking skills to become active creators of their earthly experience.

Human beings observed and explored their environments and applied their intelligence to improving their circumstances. They began to make startling discoveries about the planet's energetic styles and functions. They invented technologies, both simple and complex—from fire and the wheel to electricity and rockets—each culture creating fuller meaning and more constructive forms according to its own understanding of life.

Conscious awareness blessed the lives of earth's human inhabitants with a wealth of new opportunities. The potential for learning, understanding, imagining, inventing and discovering was limitless. With each fresh vision, insight and belief, the divine spark came alive in ways ever more vast and rich. Essence—the simple, creative source of all life—became more and more expressive and tangible with each new thought, with every fresh idea, with each innovative invention.

Human beings, now consciously aware, could realize the very divinity of their own nature, know firsthand the infinite essence that lives richly in all forms of life, and rejoice in the wonder of creation in every moment. Indeed, they could now celebrate all life, just as God does. Finally, they could use their gift of conscious awareness to rediscover the peace of their own essence, to live in the splendor and blessings of their own light, and to revel in every one of life's energies as a divine gift.

From essence to light ... from light to energy ... from energy to love ... from love to awareness, God had taken increasingly dynamic, observable forms. Miraculously, the creator, the originator of all life, could now be intimately known and celebrated by a life form of conscious persons on a tiny planet called earth, in a small galaxy called the Milky Way, in a little region of a vast universe that co-exists among many expansive universes, all of which are but one dimension of many, in this never-ending light field called infinity.

THE HUMAN PERSPECTIVE
The Miracle of Conscious Awareness

What a remarkable invention the human species is! Infinite intelligence, in its loving and imaginative creativity, brought forth a life form—you and me—with expanded brain capacity and infused it with the gift of *conscious awareness*. As a result, here we stand with the innovative capacity to reflect, think and know ... with the conscious drive to investigate, discover and invent ... and with the expanded calling to share fully and mindfully in our divine gifts. We human beings are such a fresh approach to living, such fortunate heirs to earth's generous bounty!

Why do you suppose we've been given this enormous ability to be aware? It's one of those questions that may never be fully answered. Nonetheless, it's my personal sense that, by the very act of reflecting on our human and divine experience, and by perceiving and thinking about it in broad and insightful ways, we actually become more deeply involved participants in life—in its mysterious wonder, endless beauty and inventive power.

In short, simply by fully activating our awareness, we can know and celebrate our *essence* more intimately, treasure our *light* more vibrantly, and live in life's *energy* more richly. We enter completely into life's creative magic, both humanly and spiritually. As a result, our lives are so much richer, from their primal levels of experience to their mystical levels of grandeur.

The modern world tends to think about our amazing human awareness one-dimensionally—that it's all about managing human living. In contrast, through years of personal experience and helping others, I've come to see that there are actually three levels of consciousness that are available and possible for all of us.

These three dimensions of conscious awareness are: the *energy* level, the *light* level and the *essence* level.

Though I am about to discuss these three styles of knowing separately, in truth each of them is but a complementary facet of the others. Together—that is, when we are living powerfully in all three levels—they display on the screen of our understanding an amazing portrait of the multi-dimensional life that we live.

The Creator ... placed intelligence in soul, and soul in body, so that his creation would be the fairest and best.

TIMAEUS [4]

The greatest of all lessons is to know your self, because when you know your self you know God.

CLEMENT OF ALEXANDRIA [5]

Life is a game of awakening and the way we win is remarkably simple. We ... choose to live consciously.

TIMOTHY FREKE
AND PETER GANDY [6]

Before I invite us into these three variations of consciousness in more detail, I'd like to briefly describe each style using the analogy of a jigsaw puzzle:

- In *energy-oriented consciousness* we are aware of and relate to the individual pieces of the jigsaw puzzle of life; our focus is strongly on individuality, separateness and differences.

- In *light-oriented consciousness* we are aware of and relate to the puzzle of life as a unified, interconnected, integrated whole; we see not the individual pieces, but the puzzle picture in its entirety.

- In *essence-oriented consciousness* we are aware of and relate to the very essence of the puzzle picture; we connect to the soul and pure being of the puzzle's content and grasp its underlying spirit.

To make the point even more tangible, I'm inviting you to yet another comparison—this time we picture life as a forest:

- At the *energy* level of awareness, we're preoccupied with making life's activities inside the forest as effective, rich and rewarding as possible.

- At the *light* level, perched happily above the forest, we see the wisdom and interconnection of everything that's happening within the forest and, from this vantage point, also enjoy the clear, vast view of life beyond the forest.

- At the *essence* level, we're hanging out solidly in a state of being—way beyond the forest's intrigues—savoring the essence and true spirit of the forest's dynamics. The deeper truth of life, both in and beyond the forest, lives strongly in us, with a state of profound peacefulness presiding over all awareness.

And here is one last simplified description:

- In *energy* awareness, we become the *I-ness* of separate-ness.

- In *light* awareness, we become the *one-ness* of all-ness.

- In *essence* awareness, we become the *is-ness* of one-ness.

Now that we're saturated with analogies, I'd like to emphasize a point that I've strongly implied above: we're not stuck, trapped or lost in the regular, human mindsets or dynamics of living here on earth. And, no, we're not really cut off from other dimensional facets of life either. Indeed, all three styles of consciousness are deeply instilled in our human make-up. All of them together are available to you and me, and make our human and spiritual experience here richer and more fulfilling.

Please keep in mind that each of these levels of consciousness—energy, light and essence—strongly invites you and me, and every human being, to play in its unique and special gifts. To deny ourselves the experience of any one of them detaches us from its abundant treasures.

Join me, then, as we explore each of these realms of awareness more deeply.

THE ENERGY DIMENSION OF AWARENESS:
BEING FULLY HUMAN

All of us come to earth, I deeply believe, with an innate calling: to be all that we can be. Even if we choose to shrink from that core calling at times, our soulful source predictably nudges us to embrace it anew. In short, being human means making the best and most of all the gifts that we have, and all of us are geared to keep responding to this spiritual urge, no matter how difficult the path or discouraging the seeming failures.

With this potent tool called consciousness, we have every means we need to fulfill this internal calling. Our awareness enables us to become empowered, engaged players in our daily circumstances ... make effective choices in building our lives ... and participate actively in manifesting our fulfillment. Yes, we possess enormous potential for endless achievement, personal growth and creative richness. Our consciousness is our perfect ticket to achieving anything that is humanly possible.

THE REMARKABLE QUALITIES OF ENERGY CONSCIOUSNESS

In one sense, it's unnecessary to describe our "regular" human mind and its impressive gifts. Every one of us uses the resources of our consciousness and enjoys its benefits thousands of time each day—often to the point of taking them for granted. I'd like to share with you a brief perspective of this enormous gift, though, simply because most of us have lost a loving relationship with it in our daily rituals of human living.

Our separateness is an illusion; we are interconnected parts of the whole.

ERVIN LASZLO [10]

I am the God which creates in the head of man the fire of thought. Who will enlighten each question if not I?

THE HEROIC CYCLE [11]

Our reality is larger than you and me, and all the vessels that sail the waters, and all the waters on which they sail.

ERVIN LASZLO [12]

It is the food which you furnish to your mind that determines the whole character of your life.

EMMET FOX [13]

Reality is not just the physical world; it's the relationship of the mind with the physical world that creates the perception of reality. There's no reality without a perception of reality.

FRED ALAN WOLF [14]

Any sufficiently advanced technology is indistinguishable from magic.

ARTHUR C CLARKE [15]

Imagine yourself, if you will, as having newly arrived in our world—shortly after your cosmic travel agent convinced you to come to earth for your well-deserved vacation. With few preconceptions about how life works on this planet, you look around, and what do you see?

First you notice how inventive your fellow human beings are. You see them identifying and interpreting challenges, weighing their options and responding with creative decisions.

You observe how they philosophize about life, construct theories and build beliefs. Then you look more closely and see how they treasure their learned values, apply their principles for constructive living, and interrelate one idea with another until they actually evolve a totally new thought. Finally, you survey the world around you for the effects of this creative cognitive gift ... and you behold the striking inventions, extraordinary discoveries and mind-boggling innovations that surround you, demonstrating humanity's creative genius. "Very impressive!" you think to yourself.

So, it's clear: with our inventive human intellect and active awareness, you and I can create our lives with purpose and meaning, both individually and collectively. With intentional use of our gifted minds, we can attain personal decisiveness and creative mastery. We can literally fashion lives of unbounded possibilities, never-ending discoveries and infinitely rich fulfillment—and thereby achieve our largest purposes as human beings. What a marvelous resource we have in our human treasure chest!

Indeed, we have every right to be in awe of this amazing treasure that we inherited upon our entry into this three-dimensional earth. Even if simply for solving our daily human dilemmas and challenges, energy-oriented consciousness serves us with dedication, commitment and support. With a full embrace of this powerful consciousness, we are truly masters of our destiny.

WHEN IT'S TIME TO MOVE ON

And there's even better news. At some point, this human intellect of ours, extraordinary and supportive as it is in managing our energy-filled world, begins to feel limited, or too restrictive, or just plain boring. After all, since it is only one part of an impressive three-piece system of awareness, it's not designed to operate in isolation, but as an intricate component of a larger whole.

So, there comes a time in each of our lives when, from the deeper resources of our wisdom-filled soul, we feel a bigger calling: the inner urge to open ourselves to the more expansive consciousness that has been waiting respectfully for our attention. Our soulful wisdom now calls us to open our vision and expand our awareness. Yes, it's time to introduce our conscious mind to its super-conscious "higher self," to enter the larger world of *light*-centered consciousness.

It's precisely at this point that many of us begin to experience what we've come to call the "death of the ego." This drama-filled ritual serves as a sort of human black hole, an empty void through which we walk— usually not by our conscious choice—as a powerful rite of passage into higher consciousness.

This rich process, which can last from months to years, usually includes some very difficult experiences: our cognitive functions decline, our prized values and treasured desires slip underground, our energy level goes flat, our life force finds a much lower gear, and, overall, we experience emptiness and nowhereness. Yes, it is a dark night of the soul.

For some reason, this unhappy process is widely accepted as a necessary element in the expansion of our consciousness. Many spiritual traditions devalue, even disdain our regular human awareness and point out the intellect's narrow limitations when compared to the expansive knowing of "higher consciousness." Consequently, these well-intentioned traditions often assume that this death of our ordinary human mind— the dark night of the soul—is the only passage to freedom.

From one point of view, of course, they are correct. If we contrast one style of consciousness against the other, there's no question about the compelling beauty, grandeur and freedom of our higher consciousness. But is it necessary to employ such a judgmental, duality-based approach when inviting ourselves into a unity-filled consciousness? I think not. In fact, it may just be time to stop making a villain of our mind (and everything else human as well!) and take a bold step into the bigger magic of light.

Here's a more love-filled approach that I think might be helpful. Imagine what would happen if we gratefully thanked our human mind for its selfless years of loyal service ... announced that we're giving it a well-deserved promotion and a new title ... and invited it into its new office with a "Higher Consciousness" sign on the door.

Now is the time to understand that all your ideas of right and wrong were just a child's training wheels to be laid aside when you finally live with veracity and love.

HAFIZ [16]

You have to go out of your mind to get into your heart.

KIRTANA [17]

The mind is its own place, And in itself can make A heaven of Hell, a hell of Heaven.

JOHN MILTON [18]

The animal was the laboratory for the evolution of man; And man must similarly be the laboratory for the creation of superman.

SRI AUROBINDO [19]

Underlying the diversified and localized gross layers of ordinary consciousness there is a unified, non-localized, and subtle layer: 'pure consciousness.'

ERVIN LASZLO [20]

God's grace is always present intimately within us, inviting and empowering us.

GERALD G. MAY, M.D. [21]

If we take this more respectful, loving approach, then we are in a perfect position to experience a much easier integration of our conscious mind with our super-conscious mind. And we have the privilege of experiencing our mind as both pieces of the puzzle of consciousness—human-based and oneness-based, energy-oriented and light-oriented. Yes, it can be that easy—all because our expanded consciousness graciously allows it to be so.

THE LIGHT DIMENSION OF AWARENESS:
THE EXPANSIVE WORLD OF UNITY

The world looks quite different when we view it through the lens of oneness rather than duality. As we know, a duality-based perception often focuses us on our own individuality, the differences between us, and the better/worse comparisons among us. In contrast, *light consciousness* allows us to see our similarities, view our shared values, and assume a perpetual win/win approach.

At that sacred moment when it's time to open ourselves to this grander perspective of light—to enter the expansive world of oneness—we find that our regular human cognitive training and learned problem-solving skills simply aren't adequate to support this leap from duality to oneness. Only the power of light consciousness itself can manage it for us. Historically, we refer to this phenomenon as "grace."

When it's time for that long-awaited leap into oneness, all we need to do is reach up into the higher, larger realms of light consciousness and invite the gifts of oneness to find us, support us and accomplish the shift for us. This expression of openness and invitation on our part is the elegant and perfect pathway. From that moment on, our larger consciousness simply takes over. Our human self can just let go, stop feeling responsible for the leap, and wait patiently and confidently for "life" (our light consciousness) to complete the job. Yes, it's that simple.

Our human cognition, from that magical point on, begins to merge with our light consciousness in a back-and-forth dance between duality and unity ... a dance that ends ultimately in a joyous integration of worlds and a beautiful view of the unity of all life.

Once there, distinctions disappear, similarities magnify. Individuality fades in importance, and our mutual interconnectedness grabs our attention. Judgments decrease, and our appreciation of the beauty of every aspect of life increases. Our earlier sense of needing safety and protection gives way to a profound feeling of oneness with all life and a deeper level of serenity, regardless of circumstances. Resting on a privileged perch above life's forest and connected to the universe's unbounded clarity, life seems, well, easier and simpler.

In this state of light consciousness, we can still elect to perceive each person's individuality if we choose, but more and more we naturally see each of us as a light-filled mirror of the other. Also, while we can decide to respond to life's challenges pragmatically, we more and more find our inner feelings at peace because they are grounded in the knowledge of our underlying unity.

TRUTH: A CRYSTAL WITH TEN THOUSAND FACES

Let's look at how our light-oriented awareness, in its remarkably vast nature, allows us to relate to the numerous beliefs, opinions and theories that exist in our human world. As we know, each and every facet of life—politics, religion, culture, relationship, God, to name just a few—has countless beliefs and interpretations associated with it. Everywhere we turn, we find people who have beliefs about it, theories about it, explanations of it, principles about it, values attached to it, and assumptions about it. Among our world's many cultures and traditions, we must hold millions of different points of view, beliefs and values about every single aspect of our shared life here on earth.

In typical energy-oriented consciousness, of course, most of us accept or believe only one perspective or paradigm about life, God or, well, anything. We're a Democrat or Republican, liberal or conservative, Catholic or Jew. In this duality-based consciousness, we usually find our niche, fit snugly into it, then let its values and beliefs guide us through life. We even find comfort in believing that our perspective is oh-so right and the opposite oh-so wrong.

In the more expansive light world of awareness, however, we are capable of entertaining virtually endless world views at the same time. We find it much more interesting, not to mention fulfilling, to entertain *many* perspectives and perceptions simultaneously rather than just one or a limiting few. We recognize that each person's or culture's understanding of life is as valid as ours, and we can embrace its value and contribution to the whole.

In short, we can look at life as a giant crystal with ten thousand faces. Our expanded awareness now allows us to see that what we call *ultimate truth* has purposely deposited bits and pieces of itself into each of our world's many cultures, social groups and philosophies ... and that the

In the heaven of Indra, there is said to be a network of pearls, so arranged that if you look at one you see all the others reflected in it. In the same way each object in the world is not merely itself but involves every other object and in fact is everything else.

SIR CHARLES ELIOT [22]

Consciousness is light, and it comes in full-quantum states. God is full-quantum light.

JOHN F. DEMARTINI [23]

I have learned so much from God that I can no longer call myself A Christian, a Hindu, a Buddhist, a Jew. The truth has shared so much of itself with me that I can no longer Think of myself as a man, a woman, an angel, or even pure soul. Existence has become so saturated with laughter, it has freed me Of every concept and image a mind could ever war with.

HAFIZ [24]

*Out of my experience ... one
fixed conclusion dogmatically
emerges ... that we within our
lives are like islands in the sea,
or like trees in the forest. The
maple and pine may whisper to
each other with their leaves. But
the trees commingle their roots
in the darkness underground,
and the islands hang together
through the ocean's bottom. Just
so there is a continuum of cosmic
consciousness, against which
our individuality builds but
accidental fences, and into which
our several minds plunge as a
mother sea or reservoir.*

ERVIN LASZLO [25]

only way to discover the fullest possible truth is to actively appreciate and embrace all of its deposited parts. It's in this spirit that the great Mahatma, Mohandas Gandhi, could proclaim to be both a Hindu and a Muslim, or that someone can identify himself or herself a believer in all religions equally.

When we appreciate, welcome and embrace the many pictures of truth, we find a level of freedom and exhilaration that we've never known before—a freedom that fills our depths, excites our soul and fulfills our life.

MOHANDAS GANDHI AND INNER PEACE

I recall reading an impressive story about Mohandas Gandhi, the noted Hindu leader. Following India's liberation from England in 1947, Muslims and Hindus were openly fighting for control of their new country, sometimes resulting in vicious injustices and killings. When a Muslim teenager killed the son of Gandhi's Hindu friend, the victim's father shared his deep emotional pain over his son's death and pervasive feelings of hatred for the Muslims with Gandhi. He then asked the Mahatma, "What can I do to soothe and heal my feelings of pain and anger?"

Gandhi looked his friend in the eye and, with love and compassion in his voice, told him, "Find the young man who killed your son, take him into your home, then raise and love him as your own son. And, if you really want complete inner healing and peace, raise him not as a Hindu but as a Muslim."

This wise advice demonstrates how liberating it can be to step beyond the comfortable but limited style of our energy-centered consciousness. Yes, once we begin living in the bigger world of light-filled awareness, then we find in our deepest inner self a place of quiet, love and oneness.

THE ESSENCE DIMENSION OF AWARENESS:
DANCING WITH THE STARS

The above description of light consciousness sounds so fulfilling, expansive and peaceful that we might assume it just can't get any better. In fact, it can—and it does.

*The real trick in life is not to be
in the know, but to be in the
mystery.*

FRED ALAN WOLF [26]

Yes, in the remarkable tri-level world of human awareness, the sky's no longer the limit. There is yet another level of awe-inspiring consciousness: a third quality of awareness that, once we live in it and it in us, offers even greater freedom and joy. I've chosen to call it *essence consciousness.*

To me, this essence-based style of living is the most wondrous of all. When we live in life's essence, we can go directly to the heart of any matter, experience the soul of any person, and thrive in the eye of any storm. No matter what the level of drama or pain in any experience, we have the option of going directly to its underlying spirit, discovering its deepest truth, and knowing its purer invitations.

"Everything's perfect!" Yes, it's with essence consciousness that such previously puzzling, even frustrating maxims now make real sense to us. We literally know the wondrous perfection of every tiny element of life. We're no longer bound by value-laden interpretations and judgments; rather, we've stepped beyond all good/bad perceptions and are free to embrace the true perfection of every moment.

Here, in the essential world of experience, we can see God in everything, feel the divine touch in all events, and literally know everything as a divine expression. Even when someone is shouting at us in rage, it's possible to experience this person as God giving us a beautiful gift, or as a facet of ourselves loving us.

Wonder, awe and celebration become our daily experience. Why? Simply because the existential angst, psychological dramas and philosophical conundrums of our energy consciousness have given way, gracefully and lovingly, to a larger, vaster "knowing." Now we simply *know* the beauty of everyone and everything ... we truly grasp life's true Garden of Eden nature ... and we firmly feel the miracle that is imbued in every aspect of existence.

It's right here in essence awareness that we discover and live in the deepest state of inner peace. We can be at peace because there are no more battles to fight, wrongs to right or problems to correct. Everything's perfect as it is all the time, so there's only one option: to live in the peace and joy of the moment.

Yes, in essence consciousness, we've rediscovered the Garden of Eden, opened our eyes to the Shangri-La of existence, found heaven on earth. Why? Not because the world has changed, but because our perception of the world has changed. It's true, of course, that "What we believe controls what we perceive." And our beliefs and perceptions are a product of the consciousness in which we live.

So if we're hanging out primarily in *energy* consciousness, we'll tend to see a world mired in conflict and pain, and wrestle with it through

Down deep in the mind and feeling of man is the mysterious godlike Essence.

PAUL BRUNTON [27]

There's really no limit to human potential and ... to what we can effortlessly achieve. The secret is to align human intelligence with the vast, organizing intelligence of nature that governs the universe. ... Aligning individual intelligence with nature's intelligence is what's called 'enlightenment.'

JOHN HAGELIN [28]

On God's own nature has been molded man's.

HADITH [29]

right/wrong debates in our minds and problem-solving tactics in our lives.

If we're living more in *light* consciousness, we'll perceive that very same world not as pain-filled and conflicted, but as a flowing pattern of events that are moving to their own intended outcome, naturally blending opposites to create their own harmony.

Finally, if our consciousness is more grounded in *essence*, we view the same world as an expression of divine perfection—as beautiful, wondrous and awe-inspiring. The perceived duality of energy and the unity of light both dissolve into the simplicity and perfection of essence.

Yes, it's not what we're looking *at* but the lens that we're looking *through* that makes the difference in what we see. Our essence-oriented lens sees the soul of everything shining through whatever is happening. That soul invites us to the simple, pure truth, nothing else.

We have moved our sense of identity and focus from the *I-ness* of energy consciousness ... to the *we-ness* and *one-ness* of light consciousness ... to the *is-ness* of essence consciousness. From this ground of being we are and remain at peace. Period.

MY OWN STORY:
EMBRACING ALL THREE STATES OF CONSCIOUSNESS

My own intimate dance with this remarkable gift of consciousness has involved many awakenings. In fact, over the years I've come to see myself and my life as a giant experiment in the art and evolution of consciousness. In this spirit, I'd like to share with you a few of my own "giant leaps forward" in this wonderful threefold world of consciousness.

• Energy consciousness

Over many years, I had meticulously educated my mind to function powerfully in my chosen professions. After degrees in philosophy, theology and psychology, and much self-study and experience in spirituality, I found that my mind had become filled to the brim with compelling ideas and knowledge—actually, much more than any one person needed. I also noticed that, no matter what was happening around me, my mind automatically produced an intelligent theory or interpretation to explain it to me.

[C]onsciousness is the ground of being; it's what is called the Godhead in Christianity and Yahweh in Judaism, and the ineffable, absolute Tao in Taoism.

AMIT GOSWAMI [30]

All the resources we need are in the mind.

THEODORE ROOSEVELT [31]

For many years, I thought this was great—my educated and astute mind left me feeling pretty smart. In fact, I thoroughly enjoyed thinking, theorizing, conceptualizing and understanding—about many subjects. Even though I had managed to keep my heart firmly in the driver's seat of my life and work, I was secretly proud of my scientific bent and intellectual prowess. Because of my strong cognitive activity, I believed that I had a real grasp on life and how it worked, felt confident in my ability to handle most situations, and enjoyed playing in life's conceptual possibilities. Ah, I was captain of my ship, indeed!

One day, something unexpectedly stirred inside me. It started as a feeling, then quickly became a tangible thought, and finally emerged as a powerful command, "Let go of all your cherished beliefs, all your prized theories and all your intelligent interpretations. Forget everything you've ever learned!"

"What?" I thought, "Forget everything I've ever learned?" You can imagine my immediate resistance to these strong words. Yet, while I certainly felt attached to the marvels of my mind and was reluctant to let them go, I began to see the wisdom in this message and decided to act on it. Even though I had no idea if there was any life after the death of all my cherished theories, I intuitively knew that it was time to empty my mind, and my internal invitation felt timely and right. So I said, "Yes!"

Here's what followed. I decided that every time my mind gave me a theory—or a belief, an interpretation or even an educated assumption—I would ignore it. That's right, I would simply not listen to its pearls of wisdom. In place of listening to those helpful thoughts, I decided that I would ignore them, "just be" with each life experience as it presented itself to me, and discover what would happen.

As I put this "letting go" process into practice, I slowly went through two powerful phases of non-thinking. The first phase was this: I began listening to ... well, nothing. That's right, what I discovered once I ventured outside the comforting and secure world of my mind's ideas was an empty void ... unfamiliar territory ... inner silence. Nothing filled the space. No thoughts or concepts came to my rescue; it was just life and me, in the raw. It was scary.

Then, after several months, came a breakthrough—the second phase. Ever so slowly, the void, the empty space, started to see some life. Now that my mind had become quiet enough, I began to sense something other than my thoughts. A quality of feeling came alive,

If a few brains are good, many brains must be better.

THE PATCHWORK GIRL OF OZ [32]

Come to the edge.
No, we will fall!
Come to the edge.
No, we will fall!
They came to the edge,
He pushed them,
And they flew.

GUILLAUME APOLLINAIRE [33]

The intellect has little to do on the road to discovery. There comes a leap in consciousness, call it intuition or what you will, and the solution comes to you, and you don't know how or why.

ALBERT EINSTEIN [34]

86

If we have no peace, it is because we have forgotten we belong to one another.

MOTHER TERESA [35]

The world and I have a common origin and all creatures and I together are one.

CHUANG-TZU [36]

You belong to everybody, And everybody belongs to you.

MAYA ANGELOU [37]

deeper than any I had ever known. I could now experience people's emotions more fully than I could remember. I came genuinely to know what others were feeling in the depths of their psyches, not because I had some theory about it, but because I actually connected energetically and empathically to their profound emotions.

But it was much more than a new level of feeling. Something deeper and fuller had happened within me. I emerged from my void fundamentally changed in my way of being present in life. I began entering into a larger world of experience—the world of …

• Light consciousness

Slowly, I stopped feeling so separate from others, and from life. I started to connect with the world around me in more intimate, sensitive ways. I felt more one with people, nature and experiences. I stopped evaluating the pros and cons of their behavior and personality traits, and began feeling others as extensions of me, and me as an extension of them.

I found myself listening—*really* listening—to people, one hundred percent. As a result, I really got what they were saying, at a gut level; I felt what they were feeling; I identified with what they were going through. I was literally living their life with them. No theory or explanation about it—just the person's experience, all by itself. I felt more intimately connected with everyone and started to enjoy richer, deeper friendships and partnerships with people—in fact, with everything in life.

It's hard to express how thoroughly changed I felt. Instead of life speaking to me intellectually, it was now touching me on the level of feeling, energy and spirit. Living became more and more an experience of the heart, of the soul, of the gut. It felt more real … I felt more real. Oneness had filled my awareness. I could never again look at a person, or hear of a tragedy, or watch the news without being instantly drawn into that person or event … without feeling deeply united with its life and invitations.

This state of light consciousness lasted for many years. During much of that time, Donna and I founded and operated the World Peace Institute in Washington, DC, a non-profit organization dedicated to creating peace, from global to personal, through what we called a "consciousness of oneness." All of life during that time spoke to me in its light-filled language of oneness. I saw the human race as the human family, humanity and the environment as one earthly presence, and the divine and the human as a reconnected reality. I viewed each person as a whole more than as an accumulation of parts, life as an integrated and vital force, and myself as an embodiment of all life. I felt deeply grateful.

- Essence consciousness

After a number of years in this expansive state of light, unexpectedly my inner light grew dimmer, my broad vision contracted, and my sense of connectedness with life ground to a halt. After a number of months, I found myself sitting in the middle of another void, even more "nowhere" than the last one.

At that point, Donna and I felt deeply inspired to take some time off from working, and lived and traveled in France for a year. During that wondrous time, I found myself living mostly in a bubble-like state of *pure being.* Once again, my whole relationship with the earth and human race changed—subtly but totally and dramatically. I now began living in the middle of humanity's soul and perceiving all of the human experience through its essence-centered eyes.

I discovered that, from this soulful center, life "just is." It is no longer perceived dualistically as good or bad, right or wrong, or even seen in its interconnected, unified dimension. No, life simply is—without any description, evaluation or commentary accompanying it. I liked this new experience; I could relate to everything, including myself, just as it was. My mind got even more of a break—with no evaluating or judging going on at all—and fell deeply in love with its new job description: to rest in each moment's invitation to *be.*

As I gradually got more used to living in life's essence, I found myself actually experiencing a remarkable quality of inner peace, more profound and real than any I had ever known. This deep state of peacefulness quickly became, all on its own, a compelling personal calling. I *had* to be at peace, no matter what. This ground of serenity, planted firmly in my core, guided my perceptions, influenced my decisions and made itself a part of my interactions from that point on.

Before I close my personal adventure in the expansive worlds of our threefold consciousness, I'd like to share one more thing with you. I discovered that, once I was firmly established in all three dimensions of awareness, I could easily and fluidly navigate among them. When I need to meet someone at an energy level, for example, I can do so, but without my essence or light consciousness shrinking or disappearing.

I welcome myself inside the inner circle where I AM and will always Be.

GEORGE E. JAMES [38]

When you take the view that there are no mistakes and accept what is, you can use your energy … to deal effectively with the situation now.

MARCI SHIMOFF [39]

Experiencing inner silence is a subtle, transcendent joy. It is a joy that comes from an underlying feeling of peace.

STEVE POSNER [40]

It's not an "either/or" but a "both/and" phenomenon: we can experience all three styles of consciousness together, in integrated and peaceful unity. So I never think of one mode of conscious awareness being better or worse, healthier or unhealthier, or more or less spiritual than another. They are all unfathomable expressions of the infinite and mysterious manifestations of the divine. I am left only in awe of it all.

THE MYSTIC PERSPECTIVE
A Tenfold Vision of Expanded Awareness

This seems to be a perfect moment to focus more visually on these three unified levels of awareness to see what expansive truths we might discover from their unique collective vision. As we open ourselves to the limitless grandeur of life and the fuller realms of knowing, we find that the three styles of consciousness blend together into a new, expanded lens through which we can perceive and know life.

For your inspiration, I would like to share a ten-fold vision that comes to me when I look at life through this integrated lens of consciousness:

1. Our experience here on earth is not nearly as central or important as we think it is. We're a small part of a much larger universe and a tiny fragment of a grander, unified truth. Most of us take ourselves and this life far too seriously, simply because we have forgotten our infinite heritage and disconnected our awareness from life's bigger realities. It's not all that serious. As author Richard Carlson might say, "It's not worth sweating the small stuff; it's all small stuff."

2. We all participate not just in this three-dimensional world, but in all of life's many dimensions. Our consciousness is an intimate part of the multi-dimensioned, though mostly invisible, realms of existence recently pinpointed by modern physicists and historically witnessed by the spiritual sages of the ages. We're not just stuck in the three-dimensional, human world of limited thought; we're a part of all life, everywhere.

3. We embody more than our familiar, narrow version of life and are already vital players in life's ultimate, unlimited realms. We are never alone. Life, in all its magnitude and largesse, is fully accessible to us and is a part of our present consciousness. Yes, at every moment, all

of life is living in and through us. Life is living us even more than we are living life.

4. We are a true and wondrous expression of God, a manifestation of divine light, an embodiment of God's wonder. We share in the divine essence and live out the utter magnificence of God. When we refer to ourselves as having a "God-Self" or "divine indwelling," we are referring to the profound ways in which divinity lives intimately within and as us. In this sense, we can indeed say "We are God" and feel whole.

5. Because of our divine heritage, we can come to know life by looking at it through the eyes of God. Yes, we can actually see life the way God does. We're not locked into limited perceptions and assumptions, but can also see and know this world through the expansive vision and pure truth enjoyed by our creative source.

6. From this divine vision, we can know—absolutely and decisively— the utter richness of everything that is happening within and around us at every moment. We see all creation as a beautiful, radiant expression of light. Like God, we have no choice but to celebrate its every manifestation. We enjoy its beauty, find peace in its perfection, and rejoice in its every expression.

7. Our locus of identity ceases to be primarily in our individuality (ego) and instead resides in life itself. Life, here on earth and encompassing the entire universe and beyond, becomes our home. We embrace ourselves as a universal being and enter the world of the mystical, which wondrously includes the practical world of the human.

8. Once established in life's expansiveness, we recognize that everything that exists or has ever existed is one. We see that separateness and individuality are simply arbitrary constructs of the human mind— convincing as they may be—and constitute only a partial version of what, in truth, is a much more infinite life. We see the bigger truth that there is only one human being, one world, one life, one everything—and each of us, like a drop of water, is a vital, radiant part of that infinite ocean. We find and enjoy the feeling of freedom that our newfound consciousness of oneness affords us.

The information field that links quanta and galaxies in the physical universe and cells and organisms in the biosphere also links the brains and minds of humans in the sociosphere. This A-field creates the human information pool that Carl Jung called the collective unconscious and Teilhard de Chardin the noosphere.

ERVIN LASZLO [43]

It really boils down to this: that all life is interrelated. We are all caught in an inescapable network of mutuality, tied to a single garment of destiny. Whatever affects one directly, affects all indirectly.

MARTIN LUTHER KING, JR. [44]

In the center of our own body,
there is a small shrine in the form
of a lotus flower, and within it
can be found a small space.
The heavens and the earth are
there; the sun, the moon and
the stars, fire and lightening
and winds—the whole universe
dwells within our heart.

THE UPANISHADS [45]

9. At the core, we are all essence—the very essence of life—and, as such, we are all connected and unified … in fact, are all the same life. Thus, when I look at someone else, I can literally see myself—no matter how different or initially repugnant that person may appear to be. I see you as a mirror of myself and all life, for the essence that we share bonds us forever in mutual love and devotion.

10. Everything, absolutely everything, is nothing more than a dreamed, imagined expression of this central essence. When we share in God's essence, we can know and become the essence of every person, situation and circumstance. Through the eyes of life's precious essence, we can know all truth. In this position, we are totally at peace—with ourselves and everything around us.

THE PHILOSOPHICAL PERSPECTIVE
What is reality?

The nature of reality is none other
than consciousness.

SEYYED HOSSEIN NASR [46]

I simply couldn't end this chapter without inviting us to visit that historically gripping question: what is the nature of reality? Why, you might wisely ask, would I want us to engage in the one question that has eluded a convincing answer for millennia and that is, inherently, so unanswerable?

Simply put, so that you can appreciate even more fully the limitless capacity of our immeasurable consciousness.

Modern science has recently turned our perceptions of reality inside out. Over the past few hundred years, we have conditioned our thinking to perceive that reality is "out there" and that it is real, objective and relatively stable. Contemporary physicists, however, are rediscovering what ancient spiritual traditions recognized: reality is in the eye of the beholder.

Yes, there is simply no external reality. The world that we see around us is nothing more than the creation of our own consciousness. Both individually and collectively, we human beings unconsciously construct the world we perceive, then convince ourselves, equally unconsciously, that it's real. Indeed, this is the basis for the current saying, "I'll see it when I believe it."

Remember that your perception
of the world is a reflection of your
state of consciousness. You are
not separate from it, and there
is no objective world out there.
Every moment, your consciousness
creates the world that you
inhabit.

ECKHART TOLLE [47]

According to this expanded view, our life here on earth is a hologram of a bigger, multi-dimensional reality … our unconscious transformation of a spiritual, mystery-based phenomenon into an apparent material form. Like Plato's shadow on the cave wall or Paul's scriptural description of earthly existence as "seeing through a glass, darkly," our human experience is a dream-like state in which we give a physical manifestation to the meanings, symbols and wonders of life.

Yet, this physical manifestation is itself an illusion of our ingenious mind. Though the illusion is persuasive, everything we see and know is but a fantasy of our inventive gift of awareness. In short, just as divine essence created light, and light generated energy, and energy in turn gave rise to conscious awareness, so our conscious awareness now daily manifests its own more concrete versions of life.

It's difficult for most of us to accept that the world that we've been taught is so convincingly real simply isn't. We have come to find a comforting sense of security in our Newtonian concept of "the reality of reality." To let go of that long-held belief and face the idea that we create our own reality here on earth ushers us into an unknown world of enormous personal accountability. How many of us are ready for such creative responsibility?

Yet, how completely freeing it can be for us to embrace this new perception! How liberating it is to see our creations as our own, our world as our personal and collective invention, and our life as simply a meaningful dream! How invigorating to know ourselves as lively creators of the story of our lives!

I believe it's like our myth of Santa Claus. In inventing this story for our children, we have taken the meaningful reality of love and created an engaging persona (Santa Claus), charming stories (Santa working in his workshop, reindeer pulling sleighs) and endearing practices (decorating trees, giving and receiving presents) to celebrate this love-powered myth. Better yet, we tell our children that Santa is real and that by believing in him they will be blessed. It's a great story, compelling ritual and meaning-filled experience.

Could it be that our earthly life is exactly the same as this wonderful tale of Santa Claus? Together, we use our vast consciousness to create the illusion of physical forms (human bodies, material world), the fantasy of important rituals (our jobs, politics and achievements), and the dream of gripping dramas (justice versus injustice, good guys versus bad guys). Finally, we conclude the story with the belief that all of this invention is very, very real—just as we do with our beloved myth of Santa Claus.

I love this phenomenon, both as we create it with the story of Santa Claus and as we recreate it many times over with the story of our lives.

Current research into the nature of the mind, and in fact into the nature of the universe itself, indicates that the universe may be nothing more than a giant hologram created by the mind.

BILL HARRIS [48]

Nothing is what it seems to be … whatever you perceive is only a kind of symbol, like an image in a dream. It is how your consciousness interprets and interacts with the molecular energy dance of the universe. An infinite number of completely different interpretations, completely different worlds, is possible and, in fact, exists … and every such focal point creates its own world, although all those worlds are interconnected.

ECKHART TOLLE [49]

We (that indivisible divinity that operates within us) have dreamed the world.

JORGE LUIS BORGES [50]

The purpose of the universe is to manifest creatively the ideas of consciousness. Manifestation is necessary for consciousness to 'see' itself and its ideas.

AMIT GOSWAMI [51]

The world is made up of stories, not of atoms.

MURIEL RUKEYSER [52]

The struggle between good and evil is the primal disease of the mind. Step aside from thinking, and there is nowhere you can't go. Don't keep searching for the truth; just let go of your opinions.

SENG-TS'AN [53]

Why do I love it? Because it demonstrates the beauty of our gift of conscious awareness, celebrates our indomitable inventive nature, and manifests the endless creative possibilities of life. It's simply a great way to "do life."

Even more, I love it because, if we can become aware that all of our experiences are simply our own creations, we can easily stay unattached to their temporary forms and give ourselves permission to create our lives differently when the time comes for a newer version. Like, perhaps, now.

Imagine with me, if you will, how you would live your life if you totally grasped that every form—your body, your personality, your job—is a holographic creation, a mythical story, a make-believe fantasy. Picture what permission you might give yourself to make new choices— to change yourself, heal your pains and re-picture your reality. It could be, and indeed would be, and in fact really is that easy, profound and wondrous.

GOOD VERSUS EVIL

Let's examine our belief in good and evil as a powerful example of our mythical creations and our innate capacity to change them.

How do we create the illusion of life? We do it, to borrow Sigmund Freud's model of human awareness, *unconsciously*—at the level of the unconscious mind.

Here, in the mysterious world of our unconscious awareness, our individuality merges with our collectivity. You and I join together with our human family—in what Carl Jung calls the collective unconscious— and we decide how to invent our experience of life. We choose the stories that we want to inform our lives.

My best guess is that early in our evolution we human beings knew that we had been given co-creative participation in God's dream. And at some point, we chose to insert an interesting element into that dream. We made this decision not rationally, but existentially, unconsciously. We somehow thought it would be a great idea to put value judgments on this dualistic experience. So, we labeled some aspects of life good and others evil, some light and others dark, some right and others wrong.

We placed these ground rules just below the surface of our awareness so that only a very few could discover and then actually change them. With this foundation in place, we set upon living out this life. And for millennia, almost all human beings have felt the grip of this setup, loving its adventure and challenges on the one hand, and feeling the weight of its self-critical judgments and painful dramas on the other.

So, for thousands of years we have been living the dream of a morally dualistic lifestyle, created by our own free will. Most of us have forgotten that the creation is entirely self-made and can easily be changed, individually and collectively.

I've spent many years helping people remember this unconscious decision, then reconnect with their primal, unconscious, creative authority and decisively make new choices about the underlying rules that govern their lives. I've watched as countless persons have found true freedom by transforming the good-versus-evil myth hidden in the depths of their psyches into a more love-filled and user-friendly set of rules such as: I can experience the basic unity of life ... or I can find the beauty of everything around me ... or, simply, I'm in charge of my perceptions at any moment ... or, even more basically, maybe I'm not so bad after all.

How about you? Are you ready to see yourself and your life as a meaningful dream or a hologram of a bigger light-filled reality? Are you ready to flow more freely and joyfully through the world that you and we have created together? Better yet, are you ready to claim the freedom to re-create it, even at the deepest levels of your unconscious mind? Are you ready to swap your good-versus-evil convictions for a freer, more liberating view of yourself and your world? You have the powerful consciousness to achieve this leap into freedom, if you feel moved to use it.

OUR PRIZED BELIEFS ... ARE SIMPLY STORIES

In the same spirit—proclaiming that our remarkable consciousness is the sole creator of our reality—I invite us to take a fresh look at our treasured world of beliefs.

As we know, many earlier societies centered their cultures around storytelling. They taught their children and grandchildren life lessons and ethical mores through fairytales, fables and myths. These stories were not intended primarily as historically accurate accounts, but rather as symbolically rich teaching tools.

I see our beliefs and attitudes in the same light, as meaningful stories that we tell ourselves, that we've gradually come to believe are right or factual or true—but aren't. Whether we choose to believe our story or

Like the Indian creator Brahma who dreams to create worlds, and the Australian aboriginal Great Spirit who dreams all of us into existence, we, too, find the source of our creative ability in our dreams. We dream in order to become aware of our future possibilities—the new ways that each of us may exist.

FRED ALAN WOLF [54]

I've always been the opposite of a paranoid. I operate as if everyone is part of a plot to enhance my well-being.

STAN DALE [55]

When we confront existence without our habitual assumptions we see our beliefs for what they are. Stories. Concepts. Words. And we see that the stories we tell about life are not life itself. Life is infinitely enigmatic. The word reality is not reality. We don't know what reality is. This radical not-knowing is the first step toward genuine knowing.

TIMOTHY FREKE
AND PETER GANDY [56]

The word genius comes from the Latin root meaning 'guardian spirit,' and that's exactly what great teachers and immortal thinkers are: creative spirits who shine light on what seems dark to others. Our own soul is the ultimate guardian spirit, and a genius is one who listens to their soul and obeys.

JOHN F. DEMARTINI [57]

Thoughts are worth having. ... And they are never worth trusting. They are never worth living for. As soon as you trust a thought ... then you cover up what is real and you can no longer see. We cannot come to that point of knowing what we do know is true until we have relinquished all of our mental constructs. ... then what is left over is what was always real.

JOHN DE RUITER [58]

not, first and foremost, from its inception to its later demise, it is simply a story, period.

All beliefs, no matter what form they take—attitudes, perceptions, interpretations, principles or theories—are stories. Granted, they may be meaningful or inspiring to us, but still they are nothing more than the stories that we've decided to value, whether we've conceived them ourselves or learned them from others.

Compare, for example, a child's way of thinking about life to that of an adolescent. Then compare the adolescent's version of truth to the adult's, and the adult's to a sage's. All of these persons hold beliefs that are important to them—and that they genuinely think are *right*—at that particular stage of life.

Yet, not one of them holds the ultimate truth about life, no matter how meaningful their convictions might be. In short, our beliefs—our stories—are always open to change, expansion and refinement. Indeed, they must change, in order to support our natural internal drive for growth.

When we let go of the notion that our beliefs are real or that they are right—and see them as simply stories that have meaning for us in this moment, we begin to experience a unique personal freedom and open ourselves to a fuller consciousness.

When we perceive ourselves as walking storytellers, we are relieved of the burden of being "right." Better yet, we are more open to changing our own story when it's time for us to move into a more expansive stage of awareness.

And so, since our infinite consciousness is totally in charge of creating our lives, and since you and I are so intimately a part of that vast consciousness, we have every right and capacity to find our deepest truth (essence) ... discover our unique place in the interconnected interplay of life (light) ... become fully the person we are created to be (energy) ... and creatively construct our reality by wisely choosing our stories (consciousness). As a result, we can bask in the unlimited spaciousness and grand possibilities of this awesome gift called consciousness.

THE PERSONAL PERSPECTIVE
Experiencing Full Awareness

Your vast threefold consciousness is a marvelous instrument for taking charge of your life, experiencing the oneness of all creation, and living in pure essence. What a gift to share humanly the infinite awareness of all the spheres! I offer the following steps to help you welcome and make the fullest use of your divine endowment of conscious awareness. As always, use them in whatever way and to whatever degree you are inspired.

STEP ONE: APPRECIATE YOUR CONSCIOUS AWARENESS

- Take a fresh look at your mind, your awareness, your consciousness. Appreciate it as you never have before. Recognize its vastness, flexibility and creativity; its artistry, logic, intuition and curiosity; its capacity for awe and analysis, reason and wisdom. Find a new sense of wonder and delight in recognizing this marvelous blessing.

- Look at your capacity to know as a special gift. See it also as a privilege, but one that carries a responsibility—the need to use it wisely, effectively, creatively and lovingly. As you open to a fresh relationship with your thinking, allow yourself to embrace this responsibility. In so doing, you will embrace a greater use of your mind.

- Allow yourself to feel the personal inspiration and empowerment that come from accepting both the gifts of your consciousness and your creative involvement in them.

STEP TWO: TAKE CHARGE OF YOUR CONSCIOUS AWARENESS

- Invite yourself to a large, authoritative role in relation to your awareness. Know that you are more than a passive recipient of the bequests of consciousness—you are not the servant of your mind, and your thoughts do not control you. In fact, you are in command of every thought, assumption and attitude in your awareness. You are an empowered thinker, an in-charge knower, a light-filled perceiver and a wisdom-based embodiment of consciousness to the degree that you accept this enhanced way of functioning.

- Call yourself to a strong, expansive, creative use of your mind. If your limited thinking is running your life in any way, assert yourself and proclaim that, from now on, you have authority over this part of your mind. You're in charge.

This vastness is not empty or a void or impersonal but filled with the incandescent nectar of selfless love, tender joy, and gratitude.

PRAJNAPARAMITA SUTRA [59]

STEP THREE: OPEN YOURSELF TO RECEIVE GRACE

If old patterns seem stronger than your efforts to improve your life, it's time to apply the power of consciousness to take charge of those patterns … but how do you do this?

You've reached the point where your mind, with all its knowledge and wisdom, needs extra help. Albert Einstein once said a problem cannot be solved on the level at which it was created. In fact, lasting solutions to thought-based issues do lie outside the energy-focused mind, in the larger dimensions of consciousness. Yes, any limitation in your thinking actually needs a totally outside-the-box solution, and here it is: *grace.*

Let's face it. Most of us struggle for years trying to fix or heal ourselves and our seeming problems. Whatever their nature, the path towards their unraveling is often tedious and time consuming. Grace can bypass that lengthy, complex process and give us what we need much more immediately.

Yet I know that, as much as we want a grace-induced miracle, a divine intervention to make the radical difference for us, many of us carry subconscious stories that simply don't allow us to receive graces' gifts. We may feel undeserving or harbor an inner sense of shame or guilt that prevents the blessing from entering fully into our experience. For these reasons and many more, we sometimes give up; we stop reaching out for the help, the grace that we need.

- Open yourself to grace. Remind yourself that grace's gifts are your birthright, that you deserve them, that you have a right to their blessings. Invite yourself to feel that deservingness within your depths.

- Be receptive. Be really, really receptive. Move beyond any subconscious stories that may have limited your receptivity to blessings in the past. If appropriate, repeat these words as frequently as you like: *I am open and receptive to grace and its love-filled gifts, now and every day of my life.*

- Connect with an infinite presence. Ask for divine love to fill your consciousness now. Become aware of God's willingness to touch any and every element of your life and make the total difference, now. Feel God within, in your own way.

- Ask for divine intervention—grace!—right now. Remember, since God is your essence, God's help is your birthright; it's already in you. Since God's life fills your veins, God's intervention is readily accessible to you at every moment.

- With all your heart, from the depths of your soul, with every ounce of your awareness, feel grace flowing into you. Sense your own now-heightened receptivity to its loving gifts. Visualize all your inner doors open wide and grace's abundant blessings pouring through them and filling your body, your emotions, your mind, your everything. Feel the full, precious, beautiful, nourishing presence of grace.

STEP FOUR: INVITE GRACE TO PARTICIPATE ACTIVELY IN YOUR LIFE

In the last step, you opened yourself to receive grace from the depths of your heart. Now, it's time for a more proactive approach—time to take charge and powerfully call grace into your life. Oh, and yes, you do deserve to take this step.

- Invite grace completely and actively into your life. Being fully present and focused, call the blessings that you need into your life, now. Simply require that you and grace meet, in the intimate playground of your life, here and now. Feel free to do this verbally (out loud), internally (silently) or in any way that feels real and genuine to you.

- Be totally open to the possibility that grace's blessings and expressions may not appear in your life in just the way you think they should. As we know, grace's inherent wisdom always creates the perfect manifestation for every moment. If you feel it would be helpful, actively invite yourself to welcome a response that may look different from what you're expecting. Or let go of any specific expectations altogether.

- Between the moment of your calling grace into action and its tangible response, repeat these words as often as you want: *Grace is now alive within me. Grace is now creating the perfect response to my need. In the meantime, grace loves me fully. I'm at peace.*

- Make it a daily practice not only to invite grace's direct participation in your life, but also to require and welcome it. Invite yourself to notice and celebrate how every minute of your day is already filled with God's presence, God's miracles, God's intervention, God's partnership and God's love.

STEP FIVE: BE GRACE

- Be grace. Once you actually require grace to become an intimate part of your life, you are ready for this ultimate step in human living—literally, to be grace. Become not only a strongly motivated participant in grace's beautiful involvement in your life, but also a strong embodiment of grace itself.

- Observe and feel grace filling your body, emotions and mind with its loving power. Hang out with grace deep inside you. Be one with grace as it moves through every cell and space in your body, every twist and turn of your thoughts, every impulse and wave of your feelings. If necessary, use any metaphor that works to help make this experience real for you. Perhaps see grace as a river of light or love filling every part of you, and then become that river.

- Now invite your consciousness to recognize all the ways in which you already are that grace-filled, love-energized, profoundly rich person with infinite everything running through your veins. Look at how life's essence has manifested miraculously as you, already having saturated you with all that grace is and could ever be. Yes, see yourself as grace; it's not only in you, it is you.

- Invite yourself to celebrate this phenomenon: You embody and are grace! Let the magnificence of this reality fill your conscious awareness, your emotional energies and your mystical nature. Let yourself glorify an essential source that, in its infinite wisdom, deposited all its creative resources within you. You are grace. You are a miracle!

- I think you are the world's most beautiful creation. So does grace. Don't you think so, too?

THE INSPIRATIONAL PERSPECTIVE

- My awareness gives precious meaning to all my experiences.

- I can understand every experience from a thousand different angles.

- There are no limits to what I can know, explore and understand.

- The truths and secrets of the universe await my open mind.

- I share God's nature. The divine lives in every detail of my daily experience.

- Everyone embodies the divine qualities of love, creativity, power and truth.

- I create my own reality with my consciousness. How glorious!

- Since God is my source, God's help is my birthright. If I just ask, I will receive.

- Grace expresses infinite love and is always present in and for me.

- My life is immersed in life's healing gifts. I can truly expect and see miracles!

- Every new viewpoint and awareness fills me with excitement.

- My expansive awareness makes life such a thrilling journey!

- Through each person's uniqueness, the infinite shows up powerfully in my life.

- I am intelligent and aware. I am a real player in the events of my life.

- I can understand, discover, learn, plan and make wise choices.

- I choose to use my consciousness to fulfill my inspired purposes on earth.

- In every duality lies unity. I choose to discover that unity in everything.

- I share divine essence, light, energy and consciousness. What a blessing!

Developing the total brain and rising to higher states of consciousness is absolutely key to achieving individual fulfillment, and is the key to contributing maximum to the evolution of society—a unified field-based civilization of peace, prosperity and harmony in the family of nations.

JOHN HAGELIN [60]

Accept as a principle that there is nothing to attain, because what we are looking for, we are already ... every step you take to attain yourself is a going away ... there is nothing to gain, nothing to lose ... you will find yourself, naturally, as you were before you were born.

JEAN KLEIN [61]

LIVING THE VISION

5

THE SCRIPTURAL PERSPECTIVE
Awakening to Life

Indeed, infinite essence had created a remarkable dream. In a phantasm of creative genius, essence experienced itself in countless expressions, myriad possibilities and endless manifestations. First, essence expressed itself as bright and radiant light, then infused that light with the power to create universes in which to splash its splendor and worlds in which to express its imaginative possibilities.

In one of these worlds, earth, light's newly created energy of love brought forth a singular version of itself—a family of awareness-filled beings who shared and experienced the infinite intelligence. Innately, this human family knew its divine roots, its free nature, its playful purpose, its soulful beauty. At their core, human beings remembered who they were; they were happy.

Grateful for their conscious awareness, humans used this wondrous gift ingeniously, creating myths, stories and beliefs to explain the world and to make their earthly experience even more interesting. Their imaginative inventions of thought inspired great breakthroughs in human living, while at the same time shifting their focus away from their perfect essence and beautiful nature.

Humankind conceived creative myths about good and evil, stories about right and wrong, and ideas about how deeply shameful it is to be human. People came to believe that the two inherently innocent sides of duality were in conflict with each other. In short, they made believe that something was terribly wrong with the radiant world they shared.

Indeed, their created nature remained pure, but they could only minimally perceive it. Though their infinite light continued to radiate within the core of their human selves, they scarcely experienced it.

Then it was as if I suddenly saw the secret beauty of their hearts, the depths of their hearts where neither sin nor desire nor self-knowledge can reach, the core of their reality, the person that each one is in the eyes of the Divine.

If only they could all see themselves as they really are. If only we could see each other that way all the time. There would be no more war, no more hatred, no more cruelty, no more greed. ...

I suppose the big problem would be that we would fall down and worship each other.

THOMAS MERTON[1]

*We shall not cease from
exploration
And the end of all our exploring
Will be to arrive where we started
And know the place for the
first time.*

T. S. ELIOT [2]

*The most beautiful thing we can
experience is the mysterious.*

ALBERT EINSTEIN [3]

*I saw quite certainly ... that God
loved us before he made us; and
his love has never diminished
and never shall. And all his
works were done in this love ...
We had our beginning when we
were made, but the love in which
he made us was in him since
before time began; and in this
love we have our beginning.*

JULIAN OF NORWICH [4]

Wrapped up in their clever myths, they barely noticed the deep truth that continued to whisper its wisdom from the depths of their souls.

Throughout the ages, human beings tried hard to reawaken their awareness to their essential perfection. Through inspired religions, motivating values and guiding principles, they worked to feel less separated from God and more connected to the bigger truths of life.

In the course of these genuine efforts, something unexpected happened. In the eternal "now" of history, it was simply time for the dream of life to take its next divinely appointed step. And so, it happened: the human family began to awaken—to stir from the limitations of its self-created myths. One person at a time, people woke up to their grander, truer nature. They gradually remembered who they were, recalled their breathtaking origins, and realized that they had the power to re-create their lives. As they did, they increasingly re-connected with their created beauty. They re-discovered the awe and wonder of all creation. They recaptured their divine essence.

This unforeseen miracle was a profound expression of infinite grace, a divine intervention of gigantic proportions. This transformation of consciousness occurred not primarily as a result of any human effort, but because infinite essence chose it. With a quiet but decisive divine touch, the human dream now re-embraced its innate possibilities. Every individual could now fall in love anew with every aspect of creation.

Thus it happened that humanity completed a remarkable cycle in its creative destiny. By passing through this important ritual of forgetting and re-awakening, the human family now consciously owned its original birthright: free and full participation in its own miraculous nature.

Thus, essence's ingenious dream experienced a quantum leap forward, a leap that allowed even grander possibilities for realization and fulfillment.

Ultimately, of course, this original dream will undergo a fuller completion. All life will re-awaken unto its original essence, remembering that all its expressions—from light to energy to consciousness and all myriad creations—are happily self-contained in that essential "is-ness" that we have come to call God.

At that point beyond time and space, all imagined existence will come to its end. This current dream will be subsumed back into silent essence, and all life will once again simply "be," as it always was and endlessly is. And all will be complete.

And perhaps, just perhaps, new dreams—yet unimaginable— will begin.

THE VISIONARY PERSPECTIVE
Awakening to Expanded Life

Vision is a remarkable phenomenon. It has the power to open previously unseen doors and introduce us to unexplored possibilities. When our vision is expanded enough, it even generates quantum breakthroughs—in science and technology or in the important creations of our personal lives. It invites ingenious, bold steps forward that we couldn't even imagine without its benefits.

The vision we have been sharing throughout this book is, I hope, that expansive—gently initiating you into the personal freedoms and possibilities that your heart has been yearning for. My loving desire in offering this soulful vision to you is that it will stir your heart and excite your consciousness in ways that open new doors for *you*.

This chapter, *Living the Vision,* is not a how-to formula or instruction manual in practical living. Rather, I have written it as a further expression of soul—as the soul's way of speaking into your heart, stirring your vision and encouraging you to embrace life's magic and mystery more fully. In this chapter, I'm speaking not only to but, more importantly, *through* your inventive mind, into the rich vastness of your creative spirit. My intent here is to invite you to life's embedded miracles, its unfathomable mysteries and the wonders of soulful living.

You and I have arrived at an important point where we can now recognize a central truth of larger life: quantum breakthroughs happen not just because we will them, intend them or take charge of them, but because we let go into their waiting arms. Because we lose ourselves in their mystery-filled possibilities. Because we allow the magic of life to do precisely what it innately knows how to do when we simply allow it.

This chapter, then, is an intimate, profound, personal invitation—an invitation to yield to the vastness of life and self. It bids each of us to surrender to the innate wonder of our own essential being, the creative magic of our light-rich nature, the energy-empowered dynamism of love, and the inherent richness of our inventive awareness.

As we play together in this soulful vision, then, please experience it as your own doorway—a portal into a limitless experience of self and into

A vision is not just a picture of what could be; it is an appeal to our better selves, a call to become something more.

ROSABETH MOSS KANTER[5]

The vision that you glorify in your mind, the ideal that you enthrone in your heart, this you will build your life by, and this you will become.

JAMES ALLEN[6]

The goal of life is to make your heartbeat match the beat of the universe, to match your nature with Nature.

JOSEPH CAMPBELL[7]

If you want to build a ship, don't drum up people together to collect wood and don't assign them tasks and work, but rather teach them to long for the endless immensity of the sea.

ANTOINE DE SAINT-EXUPÉRY[8]

a sacred oneness with everything, everywhere. In fact, feel free to invite yourself to step into expansiveness itself ... and witness what happens.

THE POSSIBILITY PERSPECTIVE
Opening to all that we can be

When Jean Houston first published her book, *The Possible Human*[9], more than 25 years ago, I was entranced by its intriguing title. That suggestive name triggered visions of yet unimagined possibilities, not only for myself, but for our whole human family. It became clear to me that our previous vision and current hopes were far too limited.

With that stimulus and many others, something clicked in my creative depths. A transformational decision "happened" in my essential core—indeed, it came about all by itself, with no direct influence from my conscious thoughts. And my life quickly became dedicated to experiencing whatever is possible. Quite simply, I was now on the path of becoming *the possible human.*

The first step, I soon discovered, was to let go—to surrender to this indefinable infinity of potential, open myself to its mysterious style of creation, and be willing to be taken over by its bigger-than-life majesty. Of course, at the time I had little idea of the implications of releasing myself in this way. I only knew that "possibility" was in now charge of the person I had been ... that *I,* in my previously narrow sense of that term, was no longer in command ... and that a hugely spacious, even endless phenomenon called *life* would, bit by bit, be taking me over.

What follows is my attempt, humbly inadequate as it is, to share with you the experience of living that expansive universe.

THE VASTNESS PERSPECTIVE
Living Everywhere

You and I are human beings. Few of us would dispute that statement. Yet, as a human family we've developed an extremely narrow concept of what "human" means. Our vision of our human condition is often so limited that it leaves many people feeling contracted, restricted and constrained. We've forgotten, it seems, what humanness really means.

I've met countless persons who don't feel at home on this planet. They experience earthly existence as a confining, even strangling box in which they are trapped. They often tell me that being human doesn't

We must let go of the life that we have planned, so as to accept the one that is waiting for us.

JOSEPH CAMPBELL [10]

By confronting us with irreducible mysteries that stretch our daily vision to include infinity, nature opens an inviting and guiding path toward a spiritual life.

THOMAS MOORE [11]

To be what we are, and to become what we are capable of becoming is the only end of life.

ROBERT LOUIS STEVENSON [12]

allow their personal spaciousness enough room for expression. Thus, they feel forced to live as smaller and lesser beings than they really are. These individuals personify the term *existential angst*. You may be one of them; for many years, I certainly was.

We have come to believe, it seems, that being human means being cut off from our essence, unaware of our light, and only vaguely familiar with the wonder of our creative energies. Collectively, we've come to define that our central purpose is to navigate the practical aspects of living as masterfully as we can—and, indeed, to find our happiness and fulfillment in this pragmatic role. Meanwhile, life's bigger dimensions remain beyond our grasp.

As a small example of our disconnection from life's larger realms, we refer to our collective consciousness—the ways in which we are soulfully united with our human family and with all elements of life—as the realm of our "*un*conscious mind," implying that this expansive world is simply unavailable to our awareness or experience.

In short, while we acknowledge the mysterious, infinite, grace-filled workings of life, our understanding of them is so often diminished. We perceive them as "out there" somewhere, beyond our comprehension. Because of this narrow vision of ourselves, we can feel painfully lost, isolated and separate—from each other, from ourselves, from life itself. Yet, it doesn't have to be that way.

Indeed, in our current collective story many of us have forgotten that we are conceived in absolute perfection, that being human is an invitation to play in life's beauty, and that we are an intimate part of all creation, everywhere. We've shut ourselves off from so many of the rich gifts and blessings that are always within reach, but remain inaccessible to us, simply because our limited vision doesn't invite us to notice them.

OUR VAST SELF

Who are we then? If we are both interconnected and separate, a part of the all as well as strongly individual, what does this expanded picture of "human" look like?

My personal conviction is that *we are vast, spacious, multi-dimensional beings*. We live simultaneously in many spheres of consciousness and experience, even though our awareness may be focused on the more familiar three-dimensional world. In truth, you and I are human in two seemingly contradictory ways—in the historical, limited sense of

O Nobly Born, O you of glorious origins, remember your radiant true nature, the essence of mind. Trust it. Return to it. It is home.

THE TIBETAN BOOK
OF THE DEAD [13]

Our demons are our own limitations, which shut us off from the ubiquity of the spirit … Each of these demons is conquered in a vision quest.

JOSEPH CAMPBELL [14]

Spiritually one can never be alone. We are all connected to all other entities of the earth through the spirit-that-moves-through-all-things, and once realizing that spirit we become one with all things. There can be no loneliness.

TOM BROWN, JR. [15]

Whenever we try to pick out anything by itself, we find it hitched to everything else in the universe.

JOHN MUIR [16]

This vastness is not empty or a void or impersonal but filled with the incandescent nectar of selfless love, tender joy, and gratitude.

PRAJNAPARAMITA SUTRA [17]

There are only two ways to live your life. One is as though nothing is a miracle. The other is as though everything is a miracle.

ALBERT EINSTEIN [18]

The Tao is called the Great other: Empty yet inexhaustible It gives birth to infinite worlds. It is always present within you You can use it any way you want.

LAO TZU [19]

the term, and equally in its unbounded, interdimensional and limitless context.

Every minute of our lives, we are an active part of the universe's unlimited vastness and can find our identity in the beauty and wonder of the infinite. We are intimately connected with the vigor and life force of every human being, animal and energy of nature. With every breath, we inhale not only the nutrient-rich air or *chi* of the earth's atmosphere, but also the life-filled richness of the whole universe—in its inexhaustible, immeasurable infinity. In our thoughts, feelings and senses, we are always experiencing both the visible world and the invisible, the tangible and the intangible, the three-dimensional as well as the ultra-dimensional.

As an example, right now, whether you're aware of it or not, the genius of endless, luminescent light is actively creating you anew—and you're intimately involved in that process. At this very moment, your essence is speaking its wisdom into the inner chambers of your consciousness—and you're hearing it clearly in your depths.

In your deepest awareness, you are intimately connected to every person, circumstance and activity on this planet—and beyond. As you read this sentence, all things imaginable—whales in the depths of the oceans, life forms on other planets, events of the known past and seemingly unknowable future—are alive and being celebrated within the heights and depths of your consciousness.

Indeed, while we are here on this planet to specialize in three-dimensional living—the very reason we signed up for this earthly adventure—we are not here to disregard our participation in the bigger life from which we've come. In fact, we're here to add the human and earthly dimensions of life to the vaster worlds of creation that are already an innate part of who we are.

Existence here on earth is magnificent when we experience it as a part of life's bigger fabric. When we disengage it from this glorious mega-structure, however, or pretend that this world is all there is, living the human dimension can be lonely, difficult and even painful.

How phenomenal it is that we're an intimate, unified part of the whole of existence! Yet, I'd like to make an even more important point: *It is absolutely possible for you and me to access all these expressions of creation, all these facets of ourselves.* Yes, it's within our human nature to know our essential divinity, experience our endless light, connect with our vast universality, play in our primal earthiness, and own our full humanness—as well as to celebrate the many other aspects of this multidimensional realm in which we are privileged to live.

Even though we may have "played small" in our lives—and we all have—you and I are fully capable of knowing the depths of our own consciousness, the heights of the human experience, and the breadth of the universe. We have the capacity to experience the power of all creation, the magnificence of every creature (including ourselves), and the astonishing marvel of each life form. It's in our innermost make-up to discover the intricacies of events, the invisible realms of existence, the answers to the mysteries of multidimensional living, and the wondrous nature of our infinite source.

This inborn ability is central to the very meaning of human life. It implies that we have in our consciousness—indeed, in our very bones and human core—the innate power to sense, know and intuit everything that exists, whether "real" or imagined. It means that, through our conscious awareness and awesome human functioning, we can experience and connect with all creation—and everything before and beyond it. Nothing, absolutely nothing, is outside of our human scope.

All we need do is open our awareness to life's miraculous touch and, sooner or later, we find ourselves expanding into the vastness of life and enjoying the immensity of self. In that sacred moment, we fulfill our destiny and become the *vast human*.

THE EXPANSIVE ARENAS OF LIFE

Yes, the grandeur of life's vastness is available to all of us. To make the reality of our incalculable expansiveness as tangible as possible, I've classified it into six categories of experience—six ways in which we palpably participate in this multidimensional miracle. It's my hope that this description will make it easier for you to claim your unending wonder and magnificence.

We humans live in many intriguing worlds. The following dimensions are just as alive within each of us as they are in the vast expanse of creation. And even when we do not feel it, we are also vibrant, intrinsic and essential components of all of these arenas of life. The six spheres that constitute and fulfill our human experience are:

The purpose of life is undoubtedly to know oneself. We cannot do it unless we learn to identify ourselves with all that lives. The sum total of that life is God.

MOHANDAS GANDHI [20]

You shall know the truth, and the truth shall make you free.

JESUS [21]

We are all caught in an inescapable network of mutuality, tied in a single garment of destiny. Whatever affects one directly, affects all indirectly.

MARTIN LUTHER KING, JR. [22]

The human mind, associated with the highly evolved human brain, is a high-level articulation of the cosmic consciousness that, emerging from the vacuum, infuses all things in time and space.

ERVIN LASZLO [23]

Thinking: the talking of the soul with itself.

PLATO [24]

We are disturbed not by what happens to us, but by our thoughts about what happens.

EPICTETUS [25]

Myth is the secret opening through which the inexhaustible energies of the cosmos pour into human manifestation.

JOSEPH CAMPBELL [26]

• The Dimension of Consciousness

As we saw in the last chapter, we human beings have a remarkable privilege—we participate intimately in the vast, unified *consciousness* of life. Scientists are more and more coming to the conclusion that there is but one consciousness, and that you and I are integral parts of its mighty universal intelligence. Though we may believe that each of us is wired with a separate, individualized awareness—and our experience seems to verify this perception—the bigger truth is that cosmic consciousness itself is thinking us, perceiving us and creating us daily.

You and I are intimate elements of this unified field of consciousness. We can know its awesome power and experience our deep connection with its creative genius. Indeed, we have the capacity to access its endless truth through a remarkable gift that we live with every day—our own human mind. Yes, within the inherent brilliance of our multifaceted mind, we can attune to and celebrate every dimension of life.

Here's how we do it. We observe life's vastness through four remarkable portals—the four dynamic facets of our mind. We look through the distinctive lenses of our conscious, subconscious, unconscious and superconscious mind. Through each portal, we see a unique and special vision.

• Our *conscious* mind focuses on duality, individuality and differences. In this view, we see everything as separate. In fact, we see billions upon billions of discrete life forms—stars, humans, animals, plants, etc. Each one is different, boasting a distinctive personality. This contrast of individuals makes life interesting and colorful.

Through this creative conscious window, our existence looks convincingly tangible and real—and quite important. Whether we're solving problems, attending to our well being, or simply going about our daily business, being alive here can feel like serious business. So it's easy to feel stress and pressure as we take on life's important duties.

• Our *subconscious* mind opens our vision to myth, fantasy and play. Rather than seeing a real, serious world, we now enter into a delightful space of make-believe where life is a fun game of "Let's pretend!"

In this imagination-rich dimension, we recognize the illusion, *maya* or dream-like quality of earthly existence—it's not so real or significant after all—and see our life as an enchanting adventure to be enjoyed. Just like children engrossed in a game of tea party, we play here in a perceived Garden of Eden where we take pleasure in the creation of the moment, period.

Know ye not that ye are the temple of God, and that the Spirit of God dwelleth in you?

ST. PAUL [27]

• Our *unconscious* mind invites us to witness the mysterious, vast world of oneness. Through this more light-filled lens, all differences unify into a harmonious whole, and we experience everything in its pure state of oneness. Here, for example, we human beings come together as a blended family in our collective unconscious and co-create our destiny.

The world and I have a common origin and all creatures and I together are one.

CHUANG-TZU [28]

Our extraordinary unconscious mind also serves as an entryway into life's unending vastness, interdimensional wonder and magical, miraculous grandeur. When we peer through the lens of our unconscious mind, we experience the absolute unity of everything— our human family, all religions and philosophies, our universe and infinity itself.

• Our *superconscious* mind is the gateway to life above the forest, the world beyond time and space, where we perceive everything in its pure essence—where it "just is." Here, we clearly see the divinity in everything and everyone.

There exists only the present instant ... a Now which always and without end is itself new. There is no yesterday nor any tomorrow, but only Now, as it was a thousand years ago and as it will be a thousand years hence.

MEISTER ECKHART [29]

Sitting in this pure state of being, we have the privilege of looking directly into the heart of every person, connecting to the truth of every circumstance, and seeing the essence of every situation. We observe the absolute perfection of each moment and live in the sacred now of every event. Indeed, in this miraculous superconscious world, we have found "the peace that surpasseth all understanding." [27]

• The Dimension of the Heart

Love is everywhere we look. It is the deepest source and soulful inspiration of all creation, the earth's central energy source, and our very own human core and foundation. We are created in love, inspired and captivated by love from the instant of our conception. Love drives our decisions, influences our emotions and determines our interactions.

It is what we do with our hearts that affects others most deeply. We love from heart to heart.

MAHARISHI MAHESH YOGI [30]

In our created nature, we humans are wrapped in love's protective arms and held in her caring embrace at every moment.

The heart is a perfect poetic metaphor for this marvel called love. The entire universe pulsates to the rhythm of its expansive, resplendent heart. Our love-infused earth breathes in cadence with its own powerful heartbeat. And we human beings boast an unconditionally loving heart at our center.

Miraculously, all these hearts share the same rich quality of love and, through that singular force, celebrate the nurturing, inclusive nature of all life. Because of our radiantly alive hearts, we are eternal, active partners with love's creative power and life-giving gifts. Even when our focus is elsewhere, love remains the heart of life and our heart—our central and all-inspiring life force.

When we look at life through our embracing heart, we see love everywhere. With our heart's grand vision, we experience our divine source as love, regard each other as steeped in love, and behold the loving design of the entire universe. What a gift it is to share in this love-filled heart of life!

- The Dimension of the Body

Every quality of life, without exception, can be found in our physical world. Essence, light, energy and consciousness have all birthed themselves into the seemingly tangible, concretized form of our bodily substance. Miraculously, our human bodies contain, experience and celebrate all of creation at every moment. They daily replicate the universe's magical creative activity within their cells and express its pulsating life force in their physical fabric. Our bodies are beautiful and amazing models of life's bounteous wonder.

You and I came into this human world and took on these bodies so we could experience the mystical "all" of life in physical, tangible ways. We revel in the remarkable miracle of ongoing creation with our marvelous bodies—whether they are healthy or sick, beautiful or seemingly ugly. And though most of us have forgotten to notice, every time we experience a sensation or our sub-cellular creative genius performs its alchemy, life is speaking its truth and manifesting its power.

So, simply noticing your body's vibrations and aliveness can bring you more fully into the thrill of daily creation. Deep within your cellular framework, you are already rejoicing in the phenomenon of life, exactly as parents of a newborn baby do at the awesome birth of their child.

Your body—what a wondrous miracle it is! What a beautiful expression of God! What a glorious manifestation of infinite beauty and creative power! How privileged we are to hold infinity in our cells, creation in our bones and wonder in our skin! How splendid that this magnificent body is such an intimate part of our daily life! Contemplating this amazing gift, we can only bow down in honor of our body's very presence and respectfully utter the words "Thank you!"

I stand in awe of my body.
HENRY DAVID THOREAU [34]

• The Dimension of Earth

Divinity also expresses physically as our magical, mysterious earth. While we might view this ball spinning in space as simply one planet among many, from a more expansive perspective our earth is a vibrant, living being. We honor "her" as a feminine presence, respectfully call her *Gaia,* and experience this "mother nature" as our nurturing source of life.

Our enchanting planet embodies the radiant light of the universe, the endless energy of love, and the singular consciousness of the spheres. It glows with infinite essence and emits its loving light into the sacred space around it. And we humans are privileged to live in the chi-rich halo of that radiance—we call it the earth's atmosphere.

Yes, we all share in earth's abundant energy. We live and breathe our planet's very life force as we experience her elemental vitality through earth, air, fire and water. With each step we take on her surface, we feel the energetic touch of her embrace. At every meal, she enriches our grateful bodies with vital nutrients. With every twitch of a muscle or neural pulsing of our brain, we sense her loving movement inside us.

Indeed, we *are* the planet; the planet is us. We are one and the same.

What a joy to experience God in the caress of a gentle breeze! To taste the love of the universe in the wholesome flavors of food! To feel primal fulfillment in the breathing of earth's chi! To know the power of existence in her daily creations, and to be nurtured by the eternal embrace of Nature!

Yes, the earth is the universe, the divine and the human. Our sacred planet is alive with every one of life's gifts—and, therefore, so are we.

The woods were made for the hunter of dreams
The brooks for the fisher of song
To the hunters who hunt for the gunless game
The streams and the woods belong.

SAM WALTER FOSS [35]

Finally, he created the soul of the world, placed that soul in the center of the world's body and diffused it in every direction. Having thus been created as a perfect, self-sufficient and intelligent being, the world is a God.

PLATO [36]

*The eye with which I see God is
the same eye that sees me. My eye
and the eye of god are one eye, one
vision, one knowledge, one love.*

MEISTER ECKHART [37]

*The beginning and the end is a
primordial encounter with the
great abyss of beauty that we call
the universe. Not to enter such
moments of awe, not to live each
day ... floating inside a colossal
and intimate mystery,
is to live a life that is deprived.*

BRIAN SWIMME [38]

*Follow your bliss and the universe
will open doors for you where
there were only walls.*

JOSEPH CAMPBEL [39]

*Know ye not that ye are the
temple of God, and that the
Spirit of God dwelleth in you?*

ST. PAUL [40]

• The Dimension of the Universe

The universe. How often we utter this simple yet measureless term! We might use it to refer to the heavenly body of visible stars, or the divine source of all life, or the awe-filled wonder of life itself.

In this context, I'm referring to the universe as all of the above, but especially as life's unspeakable essence, its luminescent light, its all-pervasive energy and its remarkable consciousness—both the is-ness and all-ness of life itself.

Our amazing universe encompasses the inspiring grandeur and majesty of all dimensions. Everything we know and can imagine, and all that is yet to be discovered, conceived and created—the visible and invisible, existence and non-existence, absolutely everything—rests in the loving arms of the universe. What an awesome many-dimensional phenomenon!

You and I, like all human beings, are living, breathing parts of this multidimensional universe. We embody it within every element of our humanness—its pure essence in our soul, its luminous light in our presence, its creative possibilities in our energy field, and its loving inspiration in our awareness. This spacious universe of infinite all-ness inspires, enlivens and fulfills us every moment of our lives. Indeed, we experience its radiance in each heartbeat, breath, thought and movement.

How beautiful you are, filled with the magnificence of infinity! How blessed to be united with life everywhere! To be empowered by creation's endless dynamism! To share in the gifts of the angels and saints! How enormous we are—in our consciousness and in our daily fare—as human embodiments of this amazing universe!

• The Dimension of the Divine

We all are created in the image of God. Divinity's awesome brilliance shines within us as *our* brilliance from the moment of our conception until our last breath and beyond. Infinite source is the wellspring of our very existence, creating us anew each moment. That personalized expression of infinity that we call God is perfectly replicated in the individual selves that you and I are.

We are divine—that's the short and simple truth. Any more limited description of our human nature is only a trick of the mind and ignores this penetrating sacred reality. The awe-inspiring implication is that every characteristic we assign to our creative source—qualities such as infinite love, almighty power, healing light and intelligent creativity—are equally, abundantly and eternally ours.

Yes, God is everywhere, including every human fiber. Our every thought is divine in nature, and our every emotion expresses infinite creativity. The divine is available in our God-Self, feelable in our energetic self, imaginable in our mythical self, recognizable in our thinking self, observable in our interpersonal connections, and remarkable in our unity with all life.

What a blessing it is to share in divinity's grandeur! How fortunate we are to experience the infinite in the midst of our finiteness! And what joy in perceiving ourselves as living expressions of God's beauty and perfection! This remarkable realization—that every aspect of our humanness is divine—can be, all by itself, a life-changing and awakening phenomenon. May it be that for you, at whatever moment is perfect for you!

THROUGH THE LENS OF ...

I sometimes think about these six dimensions as unique lenses through which we look at and experience our world. Each distinctive style of perception gives us a one-of-a-kind view of this magical thing called life. For example:

- When we look through the lens of the *divine*, we see the absolute perfection of everything in creation.

- When we envision what the *universe* sees, we perceive life's compelling oneness and interconnectedness.

- When we peer through the terrestrial lens of the *earth*, we witness creation taking material form in dynamic, energy-rich, physical expressions.

- The eyes of our *body* show us the generative abundance and miraculous genius of creation in deeply personal and experiential ways.

- The view through the lens of our *heart* invites us to celebrate the inherent beauty and deservingness of everyone and everything.

When you realize how perfect everything is, you will tilt your head back and laugh at the sky.

SIDDHARTHA GAUTAMA [41]

True salvation ... is to 'know God'—not as something outside you but as your own innermost essence. True salvation is to know yourself as an inseparable part of the timeless and formless One Life from which all that exists derives its being.

ECKHART TOLLE [42]

Because we are multidimensional living beings, each of us can perceive thousands of things individually. Because we are unidimensional in spirit, we collectively perceive thousands of things simultaneously.

DON MIGUEL RUIZ [43]

*Being in the mystery, questioning,
exploring, that's all important.*

FRED ALAN WOLF [44]

*We are each at the center of the
same universe, a moving center
that is quite mysterious yet utterly
mundane. It is both who we are
and what we are.*

GABRIELLE ROTH [45]

*Everything interpenetrates
everything, and although human
nature may seek to categorize ...
and subdivide ... the universe, ...
all of nature is ultimately a
seamless web.*

THE HOLOGRAPHIC PARADIGM[46]

*The seat of the soul is there, where
the inner world and the outer
world touch. Where they overlap,
it is in every point of the overlap.*

NOVALIS [47]

- With the vision of the multi-faceted *mind,* we find ourselves in awe of the pure intelligence and grand genius of it all, and delight in our capacity to contemplate its wonder.

Each of these lenses allows us to see life in a singular, unique way, and each perspective is marvelous in and of itself. It would be a mistake, however, to assume that any one style of vision is the best, right or real version of life. Indeed, the comprehensive or full picture only emerges when we experience each dimension clearly, and then embrace all six of them together as a unified whole. Only with this *meta-*vision does the mysterious phenomenon called life finally start to make sense. And only then.

Yes, we are designed to view our existence through multiple lenses, through multi-dimensional eyes, from diverse angles. If, for example, we look at the world only through our conscious mind—the lens that we all are so strongly trained to use—we can miss the bigger context in which the fullness of life lives. Yet, when we combine all six of these remarkable lenses, we find ourselves in utter awe of creation— its inventiveness, spaciousness, creativity and wonder—and especially of that personalized version of creation called self. With such a multi-faceted vision of life, we can't help but feel fuller, richer and bigger.

Here's the good news for each of us personally. As we look increasingly through the blended lenses of these six perspectives and play more fully in their expansive dimensions, something dramatic happens for us: *We make a twofold quantum leap of consciousness.*

First, we move beyond feeling limited and small, and ease into the larger arena of *the possible human.* Then, once we have played in the magic of that intriguing field of possibility long enough, we ultimately come to experience ourself as *the vast human.*

At this point, when we find our identity as the vast human, we come home; we have found our true nature. We've completed our human search and arrived at the center of life's truth. In current psychological traditions, we often refer to this as a state of wholeness, fulfillment or actualization. In spiritual traditions, this phenomenon is often called *nirvana,* awakening, freedom, sainthood, realization or enlightenment.

This is not, however, the kind of enlightenment that takes us away from the human experience. Instead, it actually awakens us to the fullness of what being human is all about. For, indeed, being human means being fully engaged in every possible facet of existence—the divine and worldly, the intangible and tangible, the spiritual and material. It implies embracing every aspect of life, including our emotions, mind, sexuality and relationships.

Being whole, or enlightened or awakened or free, means living fully and naturally everywhere—in our own bodies and in the vast body of life, in our own thoughts and in the unified consciousness of life, in our personal creations and in the mysterious creation called life itself. In short, we live in all six dimensions—simultaneously, freely and spaciously. Now that's being human! That's being your *vast self.*

IN CONCLUSION ...

We have experienced quite a journey together through these pages. As we explored a soulful vision of life, you perhaps uncovered anew the miracle of your human self, re-discovered the utter wonder of creation, and found yourself in awe of life's mystery-filled fabric. Possibly, you understand our earthly existence more fully, simply and powerfully.

I hope you are now in a much better position to experience the pure essence of life itself, connect with the sparkling light of your own nature, live in all the abundant energies that move in and through you, and navigate the many realms of consciousness with creativity and authority. And finally, my wish is that you have embraced yourself more fully as the vast, powerful and wondrous being that you are.

It truly has been a privilege to write this book, and sheer joy to share with you this vision that has been gifted to me over the past years. My sense is that the very soul of life, in which we all share, inspired this vision, and placed its simple concepts into my mind and its expressive words onto these pages.

Most important, however, is how these words may have touched you. They will have served you well, I believe, if they have been but quiet background music to support your personal soulful vision, or if they have stimulated a deep, intimate awakening within you.

Thank you so much for picking up this book and opening yourself to the blessings that are present in its pages.

With love and devotion to you and your soulful experience of life, I leave you with this personal prayer—and a deeply intended blessing—from me to you:

May you live your own soulful version of this inspired vision forever!

May you be filled with the unending blessings of life everyday!

My favorite thing is to go where I have never been.

DIANE ARBUS [48]

One cannot help but be in awe when he contemplates the mysteries of eternity, of life, of the marvelous structure of reality.

ALBERT EINSTEIN [49]

Life is a gift.
Each breath of air a kiss.
Each sip of water a hug.
Each taste of food a blessing.
To be cherished, treasured,
to be well served.

STANLEY LAU [50]

The sky
Is a suspended blue ocean.
The stars are the fish that swim.

The planets are the white whales
I sometimes
Hitch a ride
On.

The sun and all light
Have forever fused themselves
into my heart
And upon my
Skin.

There is only one rule on this
Wild Playground,

Every sign Hafiz has ever seen
Reads the same.

They all say,

"Have fun, my dear; my dear,
have fun,
In the Beloved's divine
Game.

O, in the Beloved's
Wonderful
Game.

HAFIZ [51]

May you, in your own way, find your essence and the essence of life itself!

May your radiant light shine brightly within and around you!

May the magical embrace of love take you over, fulfilling you completely!

May the spirit of creativity abound in your life and express richly!

May grace swirl above your head daily and impart its ever-flowing gifts to you!

May your conscious awareness awaken to its grandest levels of possibility!

May you fall in love with yourself, over and over, until you have become love itself!

May the grandeur of life find you, claim you and fill you beautifully, today!

May vastness and spaciousness be your experience in every moment!

May life's mystery and wonder become your intimate friends!

May myth and merriment take over your heart and play in your mind!

May the deepest possible peace live in your soul and speak its wisdom unto you!

May life be not what you want it to be but what you deserve it to be!

May your life mirror its pure truth to you every moment of every day!

May you let go, surrender and dissolve into life itself, and thus find fulfillment!

May the mystic in you serve you well, sharing the intimate secrets of life daily!

May your experiences reflect the deepest truth of who you are, as they always do!

May your view always be vast, your perception wide and your sight clear!

And, may you be the soulful visionary you were meant to be, from this moment on!

Thank you very much.

BIBLIOGRAPHICAL REFERENCES

INTRODUCTION

1. Quote by Marcel Proust (1871–1922), French novelist, essayist and literary critic, most known as author of *In Search of Lost Time;* source of quote unknown.

2. Quote by Joseph Campbell; (1904-1987), American mythology professor, prolific writer and popular lecturer; considered an inspired authority on comparative mythology; quote taken from *The Hero with a Thousand Faces,* by Joseph Campbell, Princeton University Press, 1972, p. 386.

3. Quote by Hafiz (1329–1389), Persian (Iranian) Muslim poet and mystic, born Shams-ud-din-Muhammad; his poetry blends themes of love, mysticism and Sufism; quote taken from *Each Soul Completes Me,* poem by Hafiz; found in *Love Poems from God: Twelve Sacred Voices from the East and West,* by Hafiz, translated by Daniel Ladinsky, Penguin Group Publishing, 2002, p. 179.

PROLOGUE

1. Quote by Edgar Cayce (1877-1945), famous American psychic, healer and channeler, known as "The Sleeping Prophet" and "America's Greatest Mystic," founder of the Association for Research and Enlightenment in Virginia in 1931; source of quote unknown.

2. Quote by Rumi (1207–1273), born Jalad-ad-Din Muhammad Balkhi Rumi, famous Persian poet, Islamic jurist, theologian and mystic; quote taken from *Out Beyond Ideas,* poem by Rumi, found in *The Essential Rumi,* translated by Coleman Barks and John Moyne, HarperOne Publishing, 1995.

3. Quote by Victoria Moran, inspirational speaker, author and life coach specializing in spirituality, wellness and personal growth; quote taken from *Lit From Within: Tending Your Soul for Lifelong Beauty,* by Victoria Moran, Harper Collins Publishers, 2001.

4. Quote taken from *The Upanishads* (Indian speculation on the nature of reality and the soul), sacred Hindu Scriptures, considered the core thought of *Vedanta* ("the culmination of the Vedas"), written c. 600 BCE; quote found in *The Upanishads*, translated by Eknath Easwaran, Nilgiri Press, 1987.

5. Quote by Paul Brunton (1898–1981), born Raphael Hurst, British philosopher, mystic and guru; prolific writer about the nature of the soul and enlightenment; quote found in *Inspiration and the Overself: Volume Fourteen, The Notebooks of Paul Brunton*, by Paul Brunton, Larson Publications, 1988, p. 64.

6. Quote by John F. Demartini, inspirational speaker, author and modern philosopher, founder of the *Concourse of Wisdom School of Philosophy and Healing*; quote taken from *The Breakthrough Experience: A Revolutionary New Approach to Personal Transformation*, by John F. Demartini, Hay House, 2002, p. 37.

7. Quote from the *Gemara Shabbat*, sacred Hebrew text containing rabbinic discussions and interpretations of the *Talmud* and commentary on the *Mishna*; quote can be found in *Masekhek Shabat—Tractate Shabbos—The Gamara: The Classic Edition, with an Annotated, Interpretive Elucidation*, edited by Josaif Asher Weiss and Yisroel Simcha Shorr, Mesorah Publications Ltd., 2003.

8. Quote by Saul Bellow (1915–2005), Canadian-born American writer and novelist, winner of the Nobel Prize for Literature (1976) and the National Medal of Arts (1988), most known for his books, *Humboldt's Gift* and *The Adventures of Augie March*; quote taken from the book, *Walking in this world: The Practical Art of Creativity*, by Julia Cameron, Penguin Books, 2003.

9. Quote by St. Augustine of Hippo (354–430 AD), Christian philosopher, writer and theologian, bishop of Hippo (Algeria) and influential in the development of Western Christianity; quote first written in *Confessions of St. Augustine* in 398 AD; quote taken from *Confessions of St. Augustine: A New Translation by Henry Chadwick*, Oxford University Press, 1991.

10. Quote by Dame Rebecca West (1892–1983), born Cicely Isabel Fairfield, British writer of Scottish-Irish ancestry; noted novelist, journalist and literary critic; a foremost public intellectual of the

20th century; quote taken from the book, *Walking in this world: The Practical Art of Creativity,* by Julia Cameron, Penguin Books, 2003.

11. Quote by Lao Tzu (literally "Old Master"), 6th century BCE, ancient Chinese philosopher and central figure in Taoism, the reputed author of the *Tao Te Ching*; quote taken from *The Way of Life, According to Lao Tzu,* translated by Witter Bynner, The Berkeley Publishing Group, 1994, p. 75.

CHAPTER 1: ESSENCE

1. Quote by Krishna ("the Divine One"), a Hindu deity, sometimes seen as an avatar of Vishnu; quote found in the *Bhagavad Gita* (meaning *Song of God* in Sanskrit), a sacred scripture of Hinduism and considered a guide to Hindu philosophy, thought to be written between the 5th and 2nd centuries BCE, chapter 10.

2. Quote taken from *Zulu Creation Story,* currently displayed in the Philip Tobias Museum at the Sterkfontein Caves, The Cradle of Humankind, South Africa.

3. Quote by Meister Eckhart (1260–1328), born Johann Eckhart von Hochheim, German Christian Dominican philosopher, theologian (teaching in Paris and Cologne) and mystic (some of whose mystical teachings were condemned by the Church); quote found in *Meister Eckhart: The Essential Sermons, Commentaries, Treatises and Defense,* by Edmund Colledge, Bernard McGinn and Houston Smith, Paulist Press, 1981.

4. Quote taken from Hopi creation story, found in *In the Hands of the Great Spirit: The 20,000 Year History of the American Indian,* by Jake Page, Free Press, 2004.

5. Quote taken from *The Book of Genesis,* first book of the Hebrew Bible and first of the five books of the Pentateuch or Torah, traditionally believed to be written by Moses; quote taken from Chapter 9, verse

6. Quote by Sri Aurobindo (1872–1950), Indian philosopher, mystic and spiritual leader, who developed a spiritual practice called *Integral Yoga;* source of quote unknown.

7. Quote by Dan Millman (1946–present), athlete, professor, speaker and author; taken from *The Laws of Spirit: Simple, Powerful Truths for Making Life Work,* by Dan Millman, H. J. Kramer Publishing, 1995.

8. Quote by Chief Luther Standing Bear (1868–1939), born Ota Kte, of the Teton Lakota (Oglala Sioux) tribe, Native American writer and actor, taken from *Land of the Spotted Eagle,* by Luther Standing Bear, Bison Books, 2006.

9. Quote by Brian Swimme (1950–present), researcher, author and speaker in cosmology, evolution and religion; founder of the *Epic of Evolution Society;* quote taken from *The Hidden Heart of the Cosmos: Humanity and the New Story,* by Brian Swimme, Orbis Books, New York, 1996.

10. Quote by Paul Brunton (1898–1981), born Raphael Hurst, British philosopher, mystic and guru; prolific writer about the nature of the soul and enlightenment; quote found in *Inspiration and the Overself: Volume Fourteen, The Notebooks of Paul Brunton* , by Paul Brunton, Larson Publications, 1988.

11. Quote by Lao Tzu (literally, "Old Master"), 6th century BCE, ancient Chinese philosopher, the reputed author of the *Tao Te Ching,* the world's second most widely published book; taken from *The Way of Life, According to Lao Tzu,* translated by Witter Bynner, The Berkeley Publishing Group, 1994.

12. Quote by Rainer Maria Rilke (1875–1926), German lyrical poet and novelist, whose well-known works are marked by a mystical sense of God and death; quote taken from the book, *Walking in this world: The Practical Art of Creativity,* by Julia Cameron, Penguin Books, 2003.

13. Quote by Lao Tzu (literally, "Old Master"), 6th century BCE, ancient Chinese philosopher, the reputed author of the *Tao Te Ching,* the world's second most widely published book; taken from *The Way of Life, According to Lao Tzu,* translated by Witter Bynner, The Berkeley Publishing Group, 1994.

14. Quote by Antoine Marie-Roger de Saint-Exupéry (1900–1944), French aviator and author, most known as author of *The Little*

Prince; quote found in *Walking in this world: The Practical Art of Creativity,* by Julia Cameron, Penguin Books, 2003.

15. Quote by Joseph Campbell (1904–1987), American mythology professor, prolific writer and popular lecturer; considered an inspired authority on comparative mythology; source of quote unknown.

16. Quote by Eckhart Tolle (1948–present), Canadian (born in Germany) spiritual teacher, motivational speaker and writer on the mystical life; quote taken from *The Power of Now: A Guide to Spiritual Enlightenment,* by Eckhart Tolle, New World Library, California, 1999.

17. Quote taken from the *Manu-Smrti,* most authoritative of the books of the Hindu law code, written in 1st century BCE and attributed to the legendary first man, Manu; quote taken from Chapter 1, verses 5–7.

18. Quote by Adyashanti, noted American spiritual teacher and author specializing in non-duality; he teaches in Satsangs and is the founder of *Open Gate Sangha, Inc.*; Adyashanti is a Sanskrit name meaning "primordial peace"; quote taken from his poem *Eternal Now,* found in *Emptiness Dancing: Selected Dharma Talks of Adyashanti,* Open Gate Publishing, 2004, p. 223.

19. Quote by Eckhart Tolle (1948–present), Canadian (born in Germany) spiritual teacher, motivational speaker and writer on the mystical life; quote taken from *The Power of Now: A Guide to Spiritual Enlightenment,* by Eckhart Tolle, New World Library, California, 1999.

20. Quote by Fyodor Dostoyevsky (1821–1881), Russian novelist; most famous for his works, *Crime and Punishment* and *The Brothers Karamazov*; quote found in *Walking in This World: The Practical Art of Creativity,* by Julia Cameron, Penguin Books, 2003.

21. Quote by Don Miguel Ruiz (1952–present), Mexican author, nagual, shaman and teacher; former medical doctor and surgeon; most known for his best-selling book *The Four Agreements;* quote taken from *Toltec Prophesies of Don Miguel Ruiz,* by Mary Carroll Nelson, Council Oaks Books, 2003.

22. Quote by Carl Jung (1875–1961), Swiss psychiatrist, early student of Sigmund Freud, and founder of Analytical Psychology; source of quote unknown.

23. Quote by Henry David Thoreau (1817–1862), American naturalist, writer, transcendentalist, tax-resister and philosopher, best known for his book *Walden;* quote taken from *Conclusion* of *Walden,* by Henry David Thoreau, Everyman's Library Publishing, 2006.

24. Quote by Joseph Campbell; (1904–1987), American mythology professor, prolific writer and popular lecturer; considered an inspired authority on comparative mythology; quote taken from *The Hero with a Thousand Faces,* by Joseph Campbell, Princeton University Press, 1972, p. 386.

25. Quote by Ramana Maharshi (1879–1950), Indian sage and spiritual leader, known as the silent teacher; quote taken from *Talks With Sri Ramana Maharshi,* by Sri Munagala Venkataramiah, Sri Ramanasramam Publishing, 2006.

26. Quote taken from *The Key: And the Name of the Key Is Willingness,* published by A Center for the Practice of Zen Buddhist Meditation, P.O. Box 91, Mountain View, California 94042, 1984.

27. Quote by Alexander and Annellen Simpkins, current motivational speakers and authors in subjects of Zen, Buddhism, Taoism, Confucianism, Taekwondo and yoga; quote taken from *Simple Taoism: A Guide to Living in Balance,* by Alexander and Annellen Simpkins, Tuttle Publishing, 1999.

28. Quote by William Blake (1757–1827), noted English poet, painter, visionary and mystic; quote taken from *The Marriage of Heaven and Hell,* by William Blake, Oxford University Press, 1975.

29. Quote taken from *The Key: And the Name of the Key Is Willingness,* published by A Center for the Practice of Zen Buddhist Meditation, P.O. Box 91, Mountain View, California 94042, 1984.

30. Quote by Maharishi Mahesh Yogi (1917–2008), devoted disciple of Swami Brahmananda Saraswati, then a famous Indian Hindu guru, founder and teacher of the Transcendental Meditation technique and the TM Sidhi program, known for his efforts to create world peace; source of quote unknown.

31. Quote by Edgar Allen Poe (1809–1849), American poet, short story writer, editor and literary critic; most known for his tales of mystery and the macabre, he is considered part of the American Romantic Movement; quote taken from the poem, *A Dream Within a Dream*, by Edgar Allen Poe; found in *Edgar Allen Poe's Complete Poetical Works,* by John H. Ingram (Kindle Edition), Kindle Book, 2007.

32. Quote by Jean Klein (c. 1916–1998), Czech musicologist, doctor and teacher of *Advaita Vedanta*; quote taken from *Transmission of the Flame*, by Jean Klein, Third Millennium Publications, 1994.

33. Quote by Eckhart Tolle (1948–present), Canadian (born in Germany) spiritual teacher, motivational speaker and writer on the mystical life; quote taken from *The Power of Now: A Guide to Spiritual Enlightenment,* by Eckhart Tolle, New World Library, California, 1999.

34. Quote by Sandra Cosentino, current American leader of vision quests among the Native American traditions, and founder of *Crossing Worlds*, centered in Sedona, Arizona; quote taken from *Listening, Flow and Change*, article by Sandra Cosentino, in her April 2005 newsletter, found on her website, www.crossingworld. com.

35. Quote by Henry David Thoreau (1817–1862), American naturalist, writer, transcendentalist, tax-resister and philosopher, best known for his book *Walden;* quote taken from *A Yankee in Canada,* by Henry David Thoreau, edited by Maynard Gertler, published by American Humanist Association, 1962.

36. Quote by Dame Rebecca West (1892–1983), British novelist, journalist and literary critic, known for her feminist and liberal leanings, and considered one of the foremost literary intellectuals of the 20th century; quote taken from the book, *Walking in this world: The Practical Art of Creativity,* by Julia Cameron, Penguin Books, 2003.

37. Quote by Lao Tzu (literally, "Old Master"), 6th century BCE, ancient Chinese philosopher and central figure in Taoism, the reputed author of the *Tao Te Ching*; quote taken from *The Way of Life, According to Lao Tzu*, translated by Witter Bynner, The Berkeley Publishing Group, 1994.

38. Quote by Brenda Ueland (1891–1985), American journalist, freelance writer and teacher of writing; best known for her book, *If You Want to Write: A Book About Art, Independence and Spirit;* quote taken from the book, *Walking in this world: The Practical Art of Creativity,* by Julia Cameron, Penguin Books, 2003.

39. Quote by Eckhart Tolle (1948–present), Canadian (born in Germany) spiritual teacher, motivational speaker and writer on the mystical life; quote taken from *The Power of Now: A Guide to Spiritual Enlightenment,* by Eckhart Tolle, New World Library, California, 1999

40. Quote by Robert Browning (1812–1889), British poet and playwright, considered a master of dramatic verse and monologues, and a foremost Victorian poet; quote taken from *Paracelsus,* poem by Robert Browning, found in *The Oxford Book of English Mystical Verse,* edited by D.H.S. Nicholson and A.H.E. Lee, Acropolis Books, 1997.

41. Quote by May Sarton (1912–1995), American (born in Belgium) poet, novelist, non-fiction writer and memoirist; many of her writings are reflections of her lesbian experiences; quote taken from the book, *Walking in this world: The Practical Art of Creativity,* by Julia Cameron, Penguin Books, 2003.

42. Quote by Marianne Williamson (1952–present), noted spiritual activist, famed author, inspirational speaker, and founder of *The Peace Alliance* and *Project Angel Food;* quote found in *A Return to Love: Reflections on the Principles of "A Course in Miracles,"* by Marianne Williamson, Harper Press, 1996.

43. Quote by Heidi Hall, contemporary spiritual artist, whose art represents many sacred spiritual traditions, considered "a spiritual pioneer, a lover of Life and the Oneness of all things"; she calls her work *Artisans of Light,* and it can be found on her website, www. artisansoflight.com; quote taken from *Essence,* a poem by Heidi Hall, previously unpublished, written for this publication.

44. Quote by Sarah Ban Breathnach, current self-help author and inspirational speaker whose self-defined mission is "to remind you of all the good in your life"; quote taken from *Simple Abundance:*

A Daybook of Comfort and Joy, by Sarah Ban Breathnach, Warner Books, 1995.

45. Quote by Cynthia Lane, contemporary American spiritual counselor, inspirational writer, human motivator, retreat leader and teacher of Native American tradition; she dedicates herself to a work of "Light-filled growth, guidance and healing" which is described on her website, www.firstlighttransformations.com; quote was written for this publication.

CHAPTER 2: LET THERE BE LIGHT!

1. Quote by Moses, historically central Hebrew religious leader and lawgiver, often referred to as the most important prophet in Judaism, and presumed (though disputed) writer of the first five books of the Hebrew Scriptures; quote found in the *Book of Genesis,* the first book of the Hebrew Scriptures, chapter 1, verses 14–15.

2. Quote from *Korero O Nehera,* ancient creation story of the *Maori* people and tradition of New Zealand; source of quote unknown.

3. Quote by Plato (427–347 BCE), Classical Greek philosopher, mathematician and author; student of Socrates and teacher of Aristotle; founder of the Academy in Athens (the first institution of higher learning in the western world); source of quote unknown.

4. Quote by Don Miguel Ruiz (1952–present), Mexican author, nagual, shaman and teacher; former medical doctor and surgeon; most known for his best-selling book *The Four Agreements;* quote taken from *Toltec Prophesies of Don Miguel Ruiz,* by Mary Carroll Nelson, Council Oaks Books, 2003.

5. Quote by Ervin Laszlo (1932–present), Hungarian philosopher of science, integral theorist and classical musician, contemporary leader in the field of science and philosophy; founder of the *Club of Budapest*; taken from *Science and the Akashic Field: An Integral Theory of Everything,* by Ervin Laszlo, Inner Traditions Publishing, 2007.

6. Quote by Hafiz (1329–1389), Persian (Iranian) Muslim poet and mystic, born Shams-ud-din-Muhammad; his poetry blends themes of love, mysticism and Sufism; quote taken from *A Crystal Rim,*

poem by Hafiz, found in *The Gift: Poems by Hafiz, the Great Sufi Master,* translations by Daniel Ladinsky, Penguin Books, 1999.

7. Quote by K. C. Cole, contemporary American journalist, editor, author specializing in science and spirituality; most known for her best-selling *The Universe and the Teacup* and *First You Build a Cloud;* quote taken from *The Hole in the Universe: How Scientists Peered Over the Edge of Emptiness and Found Everything,* book by K. C. Cole, Harcourt Publishers, 2001.

8. Quote by Bill Bryson (1951–present), born William McGuire Bryson, American author of humorous books, travel books and English language books; his 2003 book *A Short History of Nearly Everything* was awarded the prestigious Aventis Prize; quote taken from *A Short History of Nearly Everything,* by Bill Bryson, Broadway Books, 2003.

9. Quote by Brian Swimme (1950–present), researcher, author and speaker in cosmology, evolution and religion; founder of the *Epic of Evolution Society*; quote taken from *The Hidden Heart of the Cosmos: Humanity and the New Story,* by Brian Swimme, Orbis Books, New York, 1996.

10. Quote by Alice A. Bailey (1880–1949), born Alice LaTrobe Bateman, English teacher of mysticism, and writer on spiritual, occult, astrological and theosophical subjects; founder of *The Arcane School* of spirituality; quote taken from *Discipleship in the New Age,* vol. I, Lucis Publishers, 1971.

11. Quote by Jacquelyn Small, contemporary inspirational speaker and author of books on soul-based psychology, trainer of health professionals in spiritual psychology, and founder of *The Eupsychia Institute* (a training and healing program); source of quote unknown.

12. Quote by Cynthia Lane, contemporary American spiritual counselor, inspirational writer, human motivator, retreat leader and teacher of Native American tradition; she dedicates herself to a work of "Light-filled growth, guidance and healing" which is described on her website, www.firstlighttransformations.com.

13. Quote by Sandra Cosentino, take from *Listening, Flow and Change*, article by Sandra Cosentino, written April 2005, found on her website, www.crossingworlds.com.

14. Quote by Emmet Fox (1886–1951), scientist, philosopher, New Thought teacher and writer; source of quote unknown.

15. Quote by Alexander and Annellen Simpkins, taken from *Simple Taoism: A Guide to Living in Balance*, by Alexander and Annellen Simpkins, Tuttle Publishing, 1999.

16. Quote by Wallace Stevens (1879–1955), American Modernist poet; taken from the book, *Walking in this world: The Practical Art of Creativity*, by Julia Cameron, Penguin Books, 2003.

17. Quote by Sandra Cosentino, current American leader of vision quests among the Native American traditions, and founder of *Crossing Worlds*, centered in Sedona, Arizona; quote taken from *Listening, Flow and Change*, article by Sandra Cosentino, written April 2005, found on her website, www.crossingworlds.com.

18. Quote by Judith Jamison, contemporary American dancer and choreographer, well-known artistic director of the Alvin Ailey American Dance Company; quote taken from the book, *Walking in this world: The Practical Art of Creativity*, by Julia Cameron, Penguin Books, 2003.

19. Quote by Francis Lucille, current spiritual teacher of Advaita Vedanta, non-duality and pure awareness; leader of spiritual retreats and intensives (www.francislucille.com); source of quote unknown.

20. Quote by Hafiz (1329–1389), Persian (Iranian) Muslim poet and mystic, born Shams-ud-din-Muhammad; his poetry blends themes of love, mysticism and Sufism; quote taken from *My Brilliant Image*, poem by Hafiz; found in *I Heard God Laughing: Renderings of Hafiz*, by Hafiz , Daniel Ladinsky, Henry S. Mindlin, and H. Wilberforce Clarke, Sufism Reoriented Publishing, 1996.

21. Quote by Ursula Sautter, contemporary German freelance writer, literary correspondent and editor, recipient of the European Online Journalism Award in 2001; quoting famous German physicist Fritz-Albert Popp (1938–present), German biophysicist, professor and author; quote found in *Ode Magazine*, July/August 2007, vol. 5, issue 6.

22. Quote by Willa Cather (1873–1947), eminent American novelist, well known for her depictions of frontier life on the Great Plains; famous for her novels, *O Pioneers!* and *Death Comes for the Archbishop;* quote taken from the book, *Walking in this world: The Practical Art of Creativity,* by Julia Cameron, Penguin Books, 2003.

23. Quote by Woodrow Wilson (1856–1924), 28th President of the United States (1913–1921); considered a leading intellectual of the Progressive Era, was president of Princeton University and Governor of New Jersey; established the League of Nations and was awarded the Nobel Peace prize in 1919; quote taken from the book, *Walking in this world: The Practical Art of Creativity,* by Julia Cameron, Penguin Books, 2003.

24. Quote by Ralph Waldo Emerson (1803–1882), American essayist, poet, philosopher and leader of the Transcendentalist Movement; quote taken from *Montaigne, or The Skeptic,* by Ralph Waldo Emerson, found in *Representative Men: The Collected Works of Ralph Waldo Emerson, vol. IV,* by Ralph Waldo Emerson (written in 1850), edited by Andrew Delbanco, Belknap Press, 1996.

25. Quote by Gautama Siddhartha (563–483 BCE), known as *the Buddha* ("the enlightened one"), famous Indian teacher, founder of Buddhism, generally recognized by Buddhists as the supreme Buddha of our age; quote taken from *Maha-Parinibbana-Sutta,* ii, sec. 33, translated by T. W. Rhys Davids, found in *Sacred Books of the East,* by F. Max Fuller, RoutledgeCurzon Publishers, 2000.

26. Quote by Albert Schweitzer (1875–1965), Alsatian physician, philosopher, theologian and musician; quote taken from the book, *Walking in this world: The Practical Art of Creativity,* by Julia Cameron, Penguin Books, 2003.

27. Quote by Neale Donald Walsch (1943–present), American spiritual writer and motivational speaker, author of *Conversations with God* and many other spiritual books; source of quote unknown.

28. Quote by Adyashanti, noted American spiritual teacher and author specializing in non-duality; he teaches in Satsangs and is the founder of *Open Gate Sangha, Inc.;* Adyashanti is a Sanskrit name meaning "primordial peace"; quote found in *Emptiness Dancing:*

Selected Dharma Talks of Adyashanti, by Adyashanti, Open Gate Publishing, 2004.

29. Quote by Ursula Sautter, contemporary German freelance writer, literary correspondent and editor, recipient of the European Online Journalism Award in 2001; quoting famous German physicist Fritz-Albert Popp (1938–present), German biophysicist, professor and author; quote found in *Ode Magazine,* July/August 2007, vol. 5, issue 6.

30. Quote by Timothy Freke and Peter Gandy, writers on mysticism and Christianity; best known for their best-selling book *The Jesus Mysteries;* quote taken from *The Laughing Jesus: Religious Lies and Gnostic Wisdom,* by Timothy Freke and Peter Gandy, Harmony Publishing, 2005.

31. Quote by Gay Hendricks (1945–present), psychologist, writer, relationship specialist and transformational speaker, founder of the *Hendricks Institute*; quote found in his personal writings; source of quote unknown.

32. Quote by Jacques Lusseyran (1924–1971), blind French Resistance leader, Holocaust survivor, teacher and author; quote taken from *And There Was Light: Autobiography of Jacques Lusseyran,* by Jacques Lusseyran, Parabola Books, 1998.

33. Quote by Marianne Williamson (1952–present), noted spiritual activist, famed author, inspirational speaker, and founder of *The Peace Alliance* and *Project Angel Food;* quote found in *A Return to Love: Reflections on the Principles of "A Course in Miracles,"* by Marianne Williamson, Harper Press, 1996.

34. Quote (presumably) by David, taken from *Psalms,* one of the three poetic books of the Hebrew Scriptures, *Psalms,*139:12.

35. Quote by Brenda Ueland (1891–1985), American journalist, freelance writer and teacher of writing; best known for her book, *If You Want to Write: A Book About Art, Independence and Spirit;* quote taken from the book, *Walking in this world: The Practical Art of Creativity,* by Julia Cameron, Penguin Books, 2003.

36. Quote by Heidi Hall, contemporary spiritual artist, whose art represents many sacred spiritual traditions, considered "a spiritual pioneer, a lover of Life and the Oneness of all things"; she calls

her work *Artisans of Light,* and it can be found on her website, www.artisansoflight.com; quote taken from *Beings of Light,* a poem by Heidi Hall, unpublished, written for this publication.

37. Quote by Don Miguel Ruiz (1952–present), Mexican author, nagual, shaman and teacher; former medical doctor and surgeon; most known for his best-selling book *The Four Agreements;* quote taken from *Toltec Prophesies of Don Miguel Ruiz,* by Mary Carroll Nelson, Council Oaks Books, 2003.

38. Quote by Marcus Aurelius (121–180 AD), aka Marcus Aelius Aurelius Antoninus Augustus (called "the Wise"), Roman emperor (161–180 AD) and Stoic philosopher; taken from *The Meditations,* (Book Ten), by Marcus Aurelius (written 167 AD), translated by Gregory Hays, Modern Library Publishing, 2003.

CHAPTER 3: THE WORLD OF ENERGY

1. Hopi Creation Story; written by Jake Page, founding editor of Doubleday's Natural History Press and author of more than forty books on the natural sciences, zoological topics, and Native American affairs; found in *In the Hands of the Great Spirit,* by Jake Page, Simon and Schuster, 2004.

2. Quote by Llewellyn Vaughn-Lee (1953–present), British lecturer and writer on subjects of Sufism, psychology and dreamwork; quote found in *Working with Oneness,* by Llewellyn Vaughn-Lee, The Golden Sufi Center, 2002.

3. Quote by Corita Kent (1918–1986), American artist, educator and Catholic nun; quote found in the book, *Walking in this world: The Practical Art of Creativity,* by Julia Cameron, Penguin Books, 2003.

4. Quote by Chief Luther Standing Bear (1968–1939), born Ota Kte in the Sioux Native American tradition; writer, actor and advocate for Native peoples; hereditary chief of the Lakota tribe; quote found in *My People the Sioux* (New Edition), by Chief Luther Standing Bear, Bison books, 2006.

5. Quote by Cynthia Lane, contemporary American spiritual counselor, inspirational writer, human motivator, retreat leader and teacher of Native American tradition; she dedicates herself to a work

of "Light-filled growth, guidance and healing" which is described on her website, www.firstlighttransformations.com; written for this publication.

6. Quote by Llewellyn Vaughn-Lee (1953–present), British lecturer and writer on subjects of Sufism, psychology and dreamwork; quote found in *Working with Oneness*, by Llewellyn Vaughn-Lee, The Golden Sufi Center, 2002.

7. Quote by Ervin Laszlo (1932–present), Hungarian philosopher of science, integral theorist and classical musician, founder of the *Club of Budapest*; taken from *Science and the Akashic Field: An Integral Theory of Everything*, by Ervin Laszlo, Inner Traditions Publishing, 2007.

8. Quote by Tukaram (c. 1577–1650), famous Indian Marathi *Sant* (saint) and devotional poet in the Hindu tradition; quote found in *The Source*, poem by Tukaram, taken from *Love Poems from God: Twelve Sacred Voices from the East and West*, translated by Daniel Ladinsky, Penguin Compass, 2002, p. 343.

9. Quote by Brian Swimme (1950–present), researcher, author and speaker in cosmology, evolution and religion; founder of the *Epic of Evolution Society*; quote taken from *The Hidden Heart of the Cosmos: Humanity and the New Story*, by Brian Swimme, Orbis Books, New York, 1996.

10. Quote by Gary E. R. Schwartz (University professor of psychology, medicine and psychiatry) and Linda G. S. Russek (President of *Heart Science, Inc.*), found in the *Foreword* to the book, *The Heart's Code: Tapping the Wisdom and Power of Our Heart Energy*, by Paul Pearsall, Broadway Publishing, 1999.

11. Quote by Eckhart Tolle (1948–present), Canadian (born in Germany) spiritual teacher, motivational speaker and writer on the mystical life; quote taken from *A New Earth: Awakening to Your Life's Purpose*, Penguin Group Publishers, 2005.

12. Quote by Mr. Fred Rogers (1928–2003), American educator, minister, songwriter and TV host; star of *The Mr. Rogers Show*; quote found in *The World According to Mr. Rogers: Important Things to Remember*, by Fred Rogers, Hyperion, 2003.

13. Quote by Masaru Emoto (1943–present), Japanese author and researcher, president of *the International Water for Life Foundation*; quote found in *Love Thyself: The Message from Water III,* by Masaru Emoto, Hay House, 2006.

14. Quote by St. Francis of Assisi (1182–1226), Italian Catholic friar, founder of the Franciscan Order, patron saint of animals and Italy; quote from the poem *Wring Out My Clothes,* by St. Francis of Assisi, found in *Love Poems from God: Twelve Sacred Voices from the East and West,* translated by Daniel Ladinsky, Penguin Compass, 2002, p. 48.

15. Quote by Llewellyn Vaughn-Lee (1953–present), British lecturer and writer on subjects of Sufism, psychology and dreamwork; quote found in *Working with Oneness,* by Llewellyn Vaughn-Lee, The Golden Sufi Center, 2002.

16. Quote by Masaru Emoto (1943–present), Japanese author and researcher, president of *the International Water for Life Foundation*; quote found in *Love Thyself: The Message from Water III,* by Masaru Emoto, Hay House, 2006.

17. Quote by Sophocles (c. 496–406 BCE), Greek poet and tragedy playwright, author of *Oedipus* and *Antigone*; quote found in *The Three Theban Plays,* by Sophocles, translated by Robert Fagles, Penguin Classics, 2000.

18. Quote by Neil Douglas-Klotz, contemporary scholar of religious studies, spirituality and psychology; co-director of the Institute for Advanced Learning in Scotland; quote found in *The Hidden Gospel: Decoding the Spiritual Message of the Aramaic Jesus,* by Neil Douglas-Klotz, Sounds True, 1999.

19. Quote by Rumi (1207–1273), born Jalad-ad-Din Muhammad Balkhi Rumi, famous Persian poet, Islamic jurist, theologian and mystic; quote from his poem *With Passion,* found in *Love Poems from God: Twelve Sacred Voices from the East and West,* translated by Daniel Ladinsky, Penguin Compass, 2002, p. 61.

20. Quote by Anaïs Nin (1903–1977), born Angela Anaïs Juana Antolina Rosa Edelmira Nin y Culmell, a Cuban-French author who was famous for her published journals; quote found in *The*

Wisdom of Women, edited by Carol Spenard Larusso, New World Library, 1992.

21. Quote by Gabrielle Roth, modern musician, dancer, author and philosopher; known as "the urban shaman," directs the theatre company *The Mirrors* and is founder of *The Moving Center*; quote found in *The Wisdom of Women*, edited by Carol Spenard Larusso, New World Library, 1992.

22. Quote by Joseph Murphy (1898–1981), New Thought author, philosopher, minister and teacher, most known for his book *The Power of your Subconscious Mind*; quote found in *Simple Abundance: A Daybook of Comfort and Joy*, by Sarah Ban Breathnach, Grand Central Publishing, 1995.

23. Quote by Annette Harris-Rain Bear, Native American writer and channel of Native Grandfathers; quote found in *Spiritual Healing, Words from Beyond: If Only You Could Hear the Stones and the Eagles*, by Annette Harris-Rain Bear, Black Diamond Publishing, 1995.

24. Quote by Fra Angelico (1395–1455), born Guido di Pietro, famous Florentine Renaissance painter, Dominican friar and mystic, known as *Il Beato* (the Blessed); quote written in the year 1513; source of quote unknown.

25. Quote by Gabrielle Roth, modern musician, dancer, author and philosopher; known as "the urban shaman," directs the theatre company *The Mirrors* and is founder of *The Moving Center*; quote found in *The Wisdom of Women*, edited by Carol Spenard Larusso, New World Library, 1992.

26. Quote by Rose Rosetree, recognized expert, inspirational speaker and prolific writer in the field of intuition and face reading; found in *Let Today Be a Holiday: 365 Ways to Co-Create with God*, by Rose Rosetree, Women's Intuition Worldwide, 2006.

27. Quote by Katherine Mansfield (1888–1923), born Kathleen Mansfield Beauchamp, New Zealand's most famous author, modernist writer of short fiction, known for her works *Miss Brill* and *The Garden Party*; quote found in *The Wisdom of Women*, edited by Carol Spenard Larusso, New World Library, 1992.

28. Quote by Kenneth Patchen (1911–1972), American poet, novelist, painter and pacifist; quote found in *What There Is,* poem by Kenneth Patchen, found in *Collected Poems,* by Kenneth Patchen, New Directions Publishing, 1969.

29. Quote by Caroline Myss, contemporary American medical intuitive, mystic, international speaker and spiritual writer; most known for her works, *Sacred Contracts* (2002) and *Anatomy of the Spirit* (1998); source of quote unknown.

30. Quote by E. E. Cummings (1894–1962), born Edward Estlin Cummings, American poet, painter, essayist and playwright, remembered as a preeminent and popular voice of 20th century poetry; quote taken from *I Thank You, God, for This Amazing Day,* poem by E. E. Cummings, found in *Xaipe,* (collection of E. E. Cummings' finest poetry) by E. E. Cummings, Liveright publishing, 1979.

31. Quote by William Blake (1757–1827), English poet, painter and printmaker; considered a genius of the Pre-Romantic Period, his literary work is known for its philosophical and mystical undercurrents; quote taken from *Auguries of Innocence,* poem by William Blake, found in *Auguries of Innocence,* by William Blake, Grossman Publishers, 1968.

32. Quote by Zitkala-Sa (1876–1938), born Gertrude Simmons Bonnin, famous Native American writer, editor, musician, teacher, activist; Native meaning of Zitkala-Sa is "Red Bird"; co-composed the first Native American grand opera, *The Sun Dance* (1913); quote taken from *The Great Spirit,* by Zitkala-Sa, found in *American Indian Stories,* by Zitkala-Sa, Hayworth Publishing, 1921.

33. Quote by Rumi (1207–1273), born Jalad-ad-Din Muhammad Balkhi Rumi, famous Persian poet, Islamic jurist, theologian and mystic; quote taken from his poem *Out Beyond Ideas,* taken from *The Essential Rumi,* translated by Coleman Barks and John Moyne, HarperOne Publishing, 1995.

34. Quote by Jamie Sams, contemporary Native American writer and speaker, member of the Wolf Clan Teaching Lodge, co-author of *Medicine Cards* and author of *Dancing the Dream;* quote found in

Sacred Path Cards: The Discovery of Self Through Native Teachings, by Jamie Sams, HarperOne Publishing, 1990.

35. Quote by Annette Harris-Rain Bear, Native American writer and channel of Native Grandfathers; quote found in *Spiritual Healing, Words from Beyond: If Only You Could Hear the Stones and the Eagles,* by Annette Harris-Rain Bear, Black Diamond Publishing, 1995.

36. Quote by Gabrielle Roth, modern musician, dancer, author and philosopher; known as "the urban shaman," she directs the theatre company *The Mirrors* and is the founder of *The Moving Center;* quote found in *The Wisdom of Women,* edited by Carol Spenard Larusso, New World Library, 1992.

37. Quote by Constance Spry (1886–1960), famous British florist, celebrity and author, sometimes described as "the Martha Stewart of mid-century Britain"; quote found in *Simple Abundance: A Daybook of Comfort and Joy,* by Sarah Ban Breathnach, Warner Books, 1995.

38. Quote by Rabinadrath Tagore (1861–1941), Bengali (Indian) poet, philosopher, social reformer and dramatist; founder of the religious society *Brahmo Samaj;* was awarded the Nobel Prize for Literature in 1913; quote found in *Gitanjali: A Collection of Indian Poems by the Nobel Laureate Rabinadrath Tagore,* by Rabinadrath Tagore, Scribner Publications, 1997.

39. Quote by Matthew Arnold (1822–1888), English poet, sage writer and cultural critic, professor of poetry at Oxford, often called the third great Victorian poet (after Alfred Tennyson and Robert Browning); quote taken from *Literary Influence of Academies,* 1864 essay by Matthew Arnold, found in *Cornhill Magazine,* vol. 10, pp. 154–172.

40. Quote by Bill Bauman (1940–present), modern day mystic, inspirational speaker and author, spiritual visionary, founder of *The Center for Soulful Living* (www.aboutcsl.com); quote taken from *The Dance of Life,* poem by Bill Bauman, found in *The Soul in Love* (a collection of inspirational poetry), by Bill Bauman, unpublished.

CHAPTER 4: THE ARRIVAL OF AWARENESS

1. Quote by Thomas Merton (1915–1968), Trappist monk, mystic and spiritual writer; quote taken from *New Seeds of Contemplation*, by Thomas Merton, New Directions Publishing, reprinted 2007.

2. Quote taken from the *Manu-Smrti*, most authoritative of the books of the Hindu law code, written in 1ˢᵗ century BCE and attributed to the legendary first man, *Manu*; quote found in chapter 1, verses 13–15.

3. Quote by Emmet Fox (1886–1951), American scientist, philosopher, New Thought teacher and writer; quote found in *The Mental Equivalent: The Secret of Demonstration,* by Emmet Fox, Kessinger Publishing, 2006.

4. Quote by Timaeus of Locri; quote taken from *Timaeus*, a treatise written c. 360 BCE by Plato (427–347 BCE), Classical Greek philosopher, mathematician and author; student of Socrates and teacher of Aristotle; founder of the Academy in Athens (the first institution of higher learning in the western world); treatise and quote found in *The Dialogues of Plato*, by Plato, Bantam Classics, 1986.

5. Quote by Clement of Alexandria (born Titus Flavius Clemens), 2ⁿᵈ Century Christian philosopher; quote taken from *Fathers of the Second Century: Hermas, Tatian, Athenagoras, Theophilus and Clement of Alexandria,* by Philip Schaff (1819–1893), available online at www.ccel.org/ccel/schaff/anf02.html.

6. Quote by Timothy Freke and Peter Gandy, writers on mysticism and Christianity; best known for their best-selling book *The Jesus Mysteries;* quote taken from *The Laughing Jesus: Religious Lies and Gnostic Wisdom*, by Timothy Freke and Peter Gandy, Harmony Publishing, 2005.

7. Quote by Amit Goswami, contemporary Indian theoretical nuclear physicist, with specialization in quantum cosmology and quantum measurement theory, taught at the University of Oregon Institute for Theoretical Physics (1968–2003), international lecturer and author; quote found in *The Visionary Window: A Quantum Physicist's Guide to Enlightenment*, by Amit Goswami, Quest Books, 2000.

8. Quote by A. Powell Davies (1902–1957), social activist, Unitarian minister, prolific spiritual and religious writer, advocate of Atomic Energy Act of 1946, champion of racial integration; quote found in *The American Commitment*, sermon by A. Powell Davies, contained in *Without Apology: Collected Meditations on Liberal Religion,* by A. Powell Davies, Skinner House, 1998.

9. Quote by Alan Harvey Guth (1947–present), American theoretical physicist and cosmologist specializing in particle theory; professor of physics at MIT; developed the idea of cosmic inflation, holds that the universe is at least 10^{23} times bigger than we can see; quote taken from *The Inflationary Universe: The Quest for a New Theory of Cosmic Origins, by* Alan Guth, Basic Books, 1998.

10. Quote by Ervin Laszlo (1932–present), Hungarian philosopher of science, integral theorist and classical musician, contemporary leader in the field of science and philosophy; founder of the *Club of Budapest*; taken from *Science and the Akashic Field: An Integral Theory of Everything,* by Ervin Laszlo, Inner Traditions Publishing, 2007.

11. Quote taken from *The Heroic Cycle*, first century BCE legend about the heroic Celtic (Irish) peoples of the Ulaid in Northeast Ireland, put in written form in the 8th to 11th century, and preserved in the 12th century books *The Dun Cow* and *The Book of Leinster*.

12. Quote by Ervin Laszlo (1932–present), Hungarian philosopher of science, integral theorist and classical musician, contemporary leader in the field of science and philosophy; founder of the *Club of Budapest*; taken from *Science and the Akashic Field: An Integral Theory of Everything,* by Ervin Laszlo, Inner Traditions Publishing, 2007.

13. Quote by Emmet Fox (1886–1951), American scientist, philosopher, New Thought teacher and writer; quote taken from *The Seven Day Mental Diet: How to Change Your Life in a Week,* by Emmet Fox, DeVorss & Company, 2003.

14. Quote by Fred Alan Wolf (1934–present), theoretical physicist and popular writer on subjects of quantum physics and consciousness, a science popularizer on several television channels; quote taken from

Dr. Quantum's Little Book of Big Ideas: Where Science Meets Spirit,
Moment Point Press, by Fred Alan Wolf, 2005.

15. Quote by Sir Arthur C. Clarke (1917–2008), British physicist,
science fiction author, inventor and futurist, host of British TV
series *Mysterious World,* most famous for his novel *2001: A Space
Odyssey;* quote found in *Profiles of the Future,* by Arthur C. Clarke,
Phoenix (Orion) Publishing, 2000.

16. Quote by Hafiz (1329–1389), Persian (Iranian) Muslim poet and
mystic, born Shams-ud-din-Muhammad; his poetry blends themes
of love, mysticism and Sufism; quote found in *Now Is the Time,*
poem by Hafiz, taken from *The Gift: Poems by Hafiz, the Great Sufi
Master,* translations by Daniel Ladinsky, Penguin Books, 1999.

17. Quote by Kirtana, contemporary American New Age singer,
songwriter, performer, student of Gangaji, songs focus on healing,
transformation and self-awareness ("music for awakening"); song
from which quote is taken is unknown.

18. Quote by John Milton (1608–1674), famous and acclaimed English
poet, prose polemicist and civil servant for the Commonwealth of
England, most well known for his epic poem *Paradise Lost* and
his treatise condemning censorship *Areopagitica;* quote found in
Paradise Lost, by John Milton, Oxford University Press, 2005.

19. Quote by Sri Aurobindo (1872–1950), Indian Hindu nationalist,
scholar, poet, mystic, evolutionary philosopher, yogi and guru;
founded the path of integral yoga; quote found in *The Life Divine,*
by Sri Aurobindo, Lotus Press, 1985.

20. Quote by Ervin Laszlo (1932–present), Hungarian philosopher
of science, integral theorist and classical musician, contemporary
leader in the field of science and philosophy; founder of the *Club
of Budapest*; quote taken from *Science and the Akashic Field: An
Integral Theory of Everything,* by Ervin Laszlo, Inner Traditions
Publishing, 2007.

21. Quote by Gerald G. May, M.D. (1940–2005), American medical
doctor, psychiatrist, professor of contemplative theology and
psychology, prolific author of books blending psychology and
spirituality; quote taken from *Addiction and Grace,* by Gerald G.
May, M.D., Harper Books, 1988.

22. Quote by Sir Charles Eliot (1862–1931), British diplomat and administrator of the British East Africa Protectorate (Kenya), British ambassador to Japan, recognized authority on Buddhism; quote found in *Hinduism and Buddhism: An Historical Sketch,* by Sir Charles Eliot, Munshiram Manoharlol Publishers, 2006.

23. Quote by John F. Demartini, inspirational speaker, author and modern philosopher, founder of the *Concourse of Wisdom School of Philosophy and Healing*; quote taken from *The Breakthrough Experience: A Revolutionary New Approach to Personal Transformation,* by John F. Demartini, Hay House, 2002, p. 139.

24. Quote by Hafiz (1329–1389), Persian (Iranian) Muslim poet and mystic, born Shams-ud-din-Muhammad; his poetry blends themes of love, mysticism and Sufism; quote taken from *I Have Learned So Much,* poem by Hafiz, found in *The Gift: Poems by Hafiz, the Great Sufi Master,* translations by Daniel Ladinsky, Penguin Books, 1999.

25. Quote by Ervin Laszlo (1932–present), Hungarian philosopher of science, integral theorist and classical musician, contemporary leader in the field of science and philosophy; founder of the *Club of Budapest*; taken from *Science and the Akashic Field: An Integral Theory of Everything,* by Ervin Laszlo, Inner Traditions Publishing, 2007.

26. Quote by Fred Alan Wolf (1934–present), theoretical physicist and popular writer on subjects of quantum physics and consciousness, a science popularizer on several television channels; quote taken from *Dr. Quantum's Little Book of Big Ideas: Where Science Meets Spirit,* Moment Point Press, by Fred Alan Wolf, 2005.

27. Quote by Paul Brunton (1898–1981), born Raphael Hurst, British philosopher, mystic and guru; prolific writer about the nature of the soul and enlightenment; quote found in *Inspiration and the Overself: Volume Fourteen, The Notebooks of Paul Brunton,* by Paul Brunton, Larson Publications, 1988.

28. Quote by John Hagelin, contemporary scientist, educator, three-time candidate for U.S. president, professor of physics at Maharishi University of Management, Minister of Science and Technology of the Global Country of World Peace, recipient of 1992 Kilby

International Award (in particle physics); quote found in *The Passion Test: The Effortless Path to Discovering Your Destiny,* by Janet Bray Attwood and Chris Attwood, Hudson Street Publishing, 2007.

29. Quote from the *Hadith,* oral traditions relating to the words and deeds of the Islamic prophet Mohammed; traditionally regarded as important tools for interpreting the Sunnah (Muslim way of life); *hadith* were put in written form in the 8th and 9th centuries; exact source of quote unknown.

30. Quote by Amit Goswami, contemporary Indian theoretical nuclear physicist, with specialization in quantum cosmology and quantum measurement theory, taught at the University of Oregon Institute for Theoretical Physics (1968–2003), international lecturer and author; quote found in *The Visionary Window: A Quantum Physicist's Guide to Enlightenment,* by Amit Goswami, Quest Books, 2000.

31. Quote by Theodore Roosevelt (1858–1919), 26th president of the United States, leader of the Progressive Movement, governor of New York; professional historian, naturalist, explorer, author and soldier; was awarded the Nobel Peace Prize in 1906; quote spoken in a speech by Theodore Roosevelt on October 12, 1915.

32. Quote taken from *The Patchwork Girl of Oz,* by L. Frank Baum, 1913, currently published by Harper Collins, 1995. A film by the same title (and based on the book) was released in 1914, produced by The Oz Film Manufacturing Company, operated by L. Frank Baum.

33. Quote by Guillaume Apollinaire (1880–1918), born Wilhelm Albert Vladimir Apollinarius Kostrowitzky, French (born in Italy to a Polish mother) lyric poet, artist, writer and art critic, credited with coining the word *surrealism;* quote taken from poem entitled *Come to the Edge,* historically believed to be written by Guillaume Apollinaire, but recently claimed to be written by modern poet Christopher Logue (in honor of Apollinaire).

34. Quote by Albert Einstein (1879–1955), German-born theoretical physicist, best known for his theory of relativity, and winner of the 1921 Nobel Prize in Physics; named Person of the Century by *Time* magazine in 1999; quote taken from *Einstein: His Life and Universe,* by Walter Isaacson, Simon and Schuster, 2007.

35. Quote by Mother Teresa (1910–1997), Albanian Roman Catholic nun, founded the Missionaries of Charity in Calcutta (India) in 1950, known for her selfless ministry to the poor, sick and dying; winner of the 1997 Nobel Peace Prize and India's 1980 *Bharat Ratna* (humanitarian award); currently beatified by the Catholic Church and called Blessed Teresa of Calcutta; quote taken from the article *Mother Teresa Reflects on Working Toward Peace,* found on the website of Santa Clara University, www.scu.edu/ethics/architects-of-peace/Teresa/essay.html.

36. Quote by Chuang-tzu (c. 369–c. 286 BCE), classical Chinese Taoist philosopher, often referred to in English as Master Chuang; famous for asserting that the world needs no government; quote found in *the Essential Tao: An Initiation into the Heart of Taoism Through the Authentic Tao Te Ching and the Inner Teachings of Chuang-Tzu,* translated by Thomas Cleary, Harper Books, 1992.

37. Quote by Maya Angelou (1928–present), born Marguerite Ann Johnson, American poet, memoirist, dancer, playwright, director, actress and civil rights leader; known for her series of six autobiographies, especially the one entitled *I Know Why the Caged Bird Sings* (1969); her volume of poetry (1971) was nominated for a Pulitzer Prize; quote taken from *A Conversation with Dr. Maya Angelou,* found on the Target (store) website, http://sites.target.com/site/en/corporate.

38. Quote by George E. James, contemporary spiritual poet, intuition teacher and healer; creator of the Perceptive Awareness Technique; quote taken from *Eternity,* a poem by George E. James, found in *Peeling the Onion: Poems of Spiritual Awakening,* by George E. James, First World Publishing, 2006, p. 91.

39. Quote by Marci Shimoff, contemporary motivational speaker, inspirational author, co-author of many of the *Chicken Soup for the Women's Soul* books, featured in the film *The Secret,* specialist in women's self-esteem, and a leading authority on happiness; quote taken from *Happy for No Reason: 7 Steps to Being Happy from the Inside Out,* by Marci Shimoff, with Carol Kline, Free Press, 2008, p. 41.

40. Quote by Steve Posner, contemporary American spiritual teacher and author, freelance writer, political and spiritual commentator,

former professor at the University of Southern California, expert on the Middle East; quote taken from *Spiritual Delights and Delusions: How to Bridge the Gap Between Spiritual Fulfillment and Emotional Realities,* by Steve Posner, John Wiley and Son, 2008, p. 65.

41. Quote reputedly by George Carlin (1937–2008), popular American comedian, known for his irreverent philosophy and quick-thinking mind, considered an icon of comedy; source of quote unknown.

42. Quote by Albert Einstein (1879–1955), German-born theoretical physicist, best known for his theory of relativity, and winner of the 1921 Nobel Prize in Physics; named Person of the Century by *Time* magazine in 1999; quote found in *Mein Weltbild* (*My Worldview,* 1931), by Albert Einstein, taken from *Introduction to Philosophy,* by George Thomas White Patrick and Frank Miller Chapman, 1935, Houghton Mifflin, p. 44.

43. Quote by Ervin Laszlo (1932–present), Hungarian philosopher of science, integral theorist and classical musician, contemporary leader in the field of science and philosophy; founder of the *Club of Budapest*; taken from *Science and the Akashic Field: An Integral Theory of Everything,* by Ervin Laszlo, Inner Traditions Publishing, 2007.

44. Quote by Martin Luther King, Jr. (1929–1968), American Baptist minister and civil rights leader, leader of the National Association of Colored People, received the 1964 Nobel Peace Prize; quote taken from *A Christmas Sermon of Peace,* delivered by Rev. Martin Luther King, Jr., found in *The Trumpet of Conscience,* book by Martin Luther King, Jr. Harpercollins, 1989.

45. Quote taken from *The Upanishads* (Indian speculation on the nature of reality and the soul), sacred Hindu Scriptures, considered the core thought of *Vedanta* ("the culmination of the Vedas"), written c. 600 BCE; quote found in *The Upanishads,* translated by Eknath Easwaran, Nilgiri Press, 1987.

46. Quote by Seyyed Hossein Nasr (1933–present), contemporary Iranian Muslim philosopher, teacher of Islamic studies at George Washington University (since 1984), scholar of comparative religions, and author of scholarly books on Islamic esoterism,

Sufism, philosophy of science and metaphysics; exact source of quote unknown.

47. Quote by Eckhart Tolle (1948–present), Canadian (born in Germany) spiritual teacher, motivational speaker and writer on the mystical life; quote taken from *The Power of Now: A Guide to Spiritual Enlightenment,* by Eckhart Tolle, New World Library, California, 1999.

48. Quote by Bill Harris, contemporary personal growth leader, motivational speaker, author, musician, founder of the Centerpointe Research institute, creator of *The Holosync Solution* program and the *Life Principles Integration Process;* quote taken from *Development Tools for Self-Mastery: The Holosync Solution, Awakening Prologue,* CD program by Bill Harris, Centerpointe Research Institute, 2004.

49. Quote by Eckhart Tolle (1948–present), Canadian (born in Germany) spiritual teacher, motivational speaker and writer on the mystical life; quote taken from *The Power of Now: A Guide to Spiritual Enlightenment,* by Eckhart Tolle, New World Library, California, 1999.

50. Quote by Jorge Luis Borges (1899–1986), Argentine writer, poet, essayist and literary critic, professor of literature at the University of Buenos Aires (1956–1970), awarded the *Prix mondial Cine Del Duca* in 1980; quote taken from *Other Inquisitions: 1937–1952,* Washington Square Press, by Jorge Luis Borges, 1966.

51. Quote by Amit Goswami, contemporary Indian theoretical nuclear physicist, with specialization in quantum cosmology and quantum measurement theory, taught at the University of Oregon Institute for Theoretical Physics (1968–2003), international lecturer and author; quote found in *The Visionary Window: A Quantum Physicist's Guide to Enlightenment,* by Amit Goswami, Quest Books, 2000.

52. Quote by Muriel Rukeyser (1913–1980), American poet and political activist, best known for her poems on equality, feminism, social justice and Judaism; her most noted piece was her 1938 group of poems entitled *The Book of the Dead;* quote taken from the book, *Walking in this world: The Practical Art of Creativity,* by Julia Cameron, Penguin Books, 2003.

53. Quote by Chien-Chih Seng-ts'an, third Chinese Chán (Zen) patriarch (606 AD) and 30th patriarch after Siddhartha Gautama (Buddha), best known as author of the poetic *Verses on the Faith Mind*; quote taken from *Verses on the Faith Mind*, by Chien-Chih Seng-ts'an, written in 606 AD, web publication by Mountain Man Graphics, Australia (www.mountainman.com.au).

54. Quote by Fred Alan Wolf (1934-present), theoretical physicist and popular writer on subjects of quantum physics and consciousness, a science popularizer on several television channels; quote taken from *Dr. Quantum's Little Book of Big Ideas: Where Science Meets Spirit*, Moment Point Press, by Fred Alan Wolf, 2005.

55. Quote by Stan Dale (1929–2007), transactional analyst, inspirational speaker and educator, personal growth workshop facilitator, author of many books on love and intimacy, founder of *Human Awareness Institute*; quote taken from *The Success Principles: How to Get from Where You Are to Where You Want to Be,* by Jack Canfield, Harper Collins Publishers, 2005.

56. Quote by Timothy Freke and Peter Gandy, writers on mysticism and Christianity; best known for their best-selling book *The Jesus Mysteries;* quote taken from *The Laughing Jesus: Religious Lies and Gnostic Wisdom*, by Timothy Freke and Peter Gandy, Harmony Publishing, 2005.

57. Quote by John F. Demartini, inspirational speaker, author and modern philosopher, founder of the *Concourse of Wisdom School of Philosophy and Healing*; quote taken from *The Breakthrough Experience: A Revolutionary New Approach to Personal Transformation*, by John F. Demartini, Hay House, 2002.

58. Quote by John de Ruiter, contemporary Canadian philosopher, inspirational speaker and spiritual author; specializing in the nature of reality, he has founded the College of Integrated Philosophy (Edmonton, Alberta); quote taken from *Dialogues with Emerging Spiritual Teachers*, by John W. Parker, Sagewood Press, 2000.

59. Quote from the *Prajnaparamita Sutra*, a series of 40 ancient and sacred Buddhist works, considered a genre of the Mahayana Buddhist scriptures, written beginning in 100 BCE and condensed around the beginning of the Common Era; *prajaparamita* translates

as "the perfection of wisdom"; quote found in *Perfect Wisdom: The Short Prajnaparamita Texts*, translated by Edward Conze, Buddhist Publication Group, 1993.

60. Quote by John Hagelin, contemporary scientist, educator, three-time candidate for U.S. president, professor of physics at Maharishi University of Management, Minister of Science and Technology of the Global Country of World Peace, recipient of the 1992 Kilby International Award (in particle physics); quote found in *The Passion Test: The Effortless Path to Discovering Your Destiny*, by Janet Bray Attwood and Chris Attwood, Hudson Street Publishing, 2007.

61. Quote by Jean Klein (1916–1998), French medical doctor, musicologist (violinist) and revered Advaita Vedanta master; quote taken from *Transmission of the Flame*, by Jean Klein, Third Millennium Publications, 1990.

CHAPTER 5: LIVING THE VISION

1. Quote by Thomas Merton (1915–1968), Trappist monk, mystic and spiritual writer; quote first written in his personal journal following and describing his personal epiphany in Louisville, Kentucky on March 18, 1958; quoted in his *Fourth and Walnut Epiphany*, taken from *Conjectures of a Guilty Bystander*, by Thomas Merton, Image Publishing,1968.

2. Quote by T. S. Eliot (1888–1965), American poet, dramatist and literary critic, recipient of the Nobel Prize in Literature in 1948; his poem *The Waste Land* has been called the most famous English poem of the 20th century; quote found in *Little Gidding*, poem by T. S. Eliot, taken from *In Four Quartets*, by T. S. Eliot, Faber and Faber, 1944, p. 59.

3. Quote by Albert Einstein (1879–1955), German-born theoretical physicist, best known for his theory of relativity, and winner of the 1921 Nobel Prize in Physics; named Person of the Century by *Time* magazine in 1999; quote taken from the book, *Walking in this world: The Practical Art of Creativity*, by Julia Cameron, Penguin Books, 2003.

4. Quote by Julian of Norwich (1342–1416), medieval English mystic, visionary and religious writer, known for her intense spiritual visions; her major work, *Sixteen Revelations of Divine Love* (1393), is considered the first book written by a woman in the English language; quote found in *Revelations of Divine Love*, by Julian of Norwich and translated by A. C. Spearing, Penguin Classics, 1999.

5. Quote by Rosabeth Moss Kanter (1943–present), current American business speaker and consultant, tenured professor of business at Harvard, named one of the 50 most influential business thinkers in the world, and has a regular column in *The Miami Herald;* source of quote unknown.

6. Quote by James Allen (1864–1912), British philosopher, inspirational writer and poet; his most influential book was the famous *As a Man Thinketh*; initiated and published a magazine called *The Epoch;* quote found in *As a Man Thinketh*, by James Allen, Peter Pauper Press, 1960.

7. Quote by Joseph Campbell; (1904–1987), American mythology professor, prolific writer and popular lecturer; considered an inspired authority on comparative mythology; exact source of quote unknown.

8. Quote by Antoine Marie-Roger de Saint-Exupéry (1900–1944), French aviator and author, most known as author of *The Little Prince*; quote found in *The Wisdom of the Sands* (originally in French as *Citadelle)*, by Antoine Marie-Roger de Saint-Exupery (posthumously published in 1948).

9. Reference is to *The Possible Human: A Course in Enhancing Your Physical, Mental and Creative Abilities,* by Jean Houston, Tarcher Publishing, 1997 (original copyright 1982).

10. Quote by Joseph Campbell; (1904–1987), American mythology professor, prolific writer and popular lecturer; considered an inspired authority on comparative mythology; source of quote unknown.

11. Quote by Thomas Moore, current American theologian, spiritual writer and inspirational speaker, most known for his book *Care of*

the Soul; quote found in *The Re-Enchantment of Everyday Life,* by Thomas Moore, Harper Perennial Press, 1997.

12. Quote by Robert Louis Stevenson (1850–1894), Scottish novelist, poet and proponent of *neo-romanticism* in English literature; quote taken from the book, *Walking in this world: The Practical Art of Creativity,* by Julia Cameron, Penguin Books, 2003.

13. Quote found in *The Tibetan Book of the Dead,* also known as the *Bardo Thodol,* composed by Padmasambhava; a description of the experiences of consciousness between human death and rebirth; quoted in *Shambhala Sun* magazine, July 2008, p. 41.

14. Quote by Joseph Campbell; (1904–1987), American mythology professor, prolific writer and popular lecturer; considered an inspired authority on comparative mythology; source of quote unknown.

15. Quote by Tom Brown, Jr. (1950–present), American naturalist, outdoorsman and writer, founder of the Tracker school in 1978; his skills and philosophy were taught to him by an Apache elder named Stalking Wolf; quote found in *Grandfather,* by Tom Brown, Jr., Berkeley Books, 1996, p. 89.

16. Quote by John Muir (1838–1914), naturalist, preservationist and nature writer; founder of *The Sierra Club;* quote found in chapter 6 of *My First Summer in the Sierra,* by John Muir, Mariner Books, 1998 (first published in 1911).

17. Quote from the *Prajnaparamita Sutra,* a series of 40 ancient and sacred Buddhist works, considered a genre of the Mahayana Buddhist scriptures, written beginning in 100 BCE and condensed about the beginning of the Common Era; *prajaparamita* translates as "the perfection of wisdom"; quote found in *Perfect Wisdom: The Short Prajnaparamita Texts,* translated by Edward Conze, Buddhist Publication Group, 1993.

18. Quote by Albert Einstein (1879–1955), German-born theoretical physicist, best known for his theory of relativity, and winner of the 1921 Nobel Prize in Physics; named Person of the Century by *Time* magazine in 1999; quote taken from the book, *Walking in this world: The Practical Art of Creativity,* by Julia Cameron, Penguin Books, 2003.

19. Quote by Lao Tzu (literally, "Old Master"), 6th century BCE, ancient Chinese philosopher and central figure in Taoism, the reputed author of the *Tao Te Ching*; quote taken from *The Way of Life, According to Lao Tzu*, translated by Witter Bynner, The Berkeley Publishing Group, 1994.

20. Quote by Mohandas Gandhi (1869–1948), known as *the Mahatma,* Indian spiritual and political leader, most known for his advocacy of non-violent resistance; quote taken from *The Essential Gandhi,* edited by Louis Fisher, Random House, 1962, p. 316.

21. Quote by Jesus of Nazareth (7–2 BCE to 26–36 AD), known as *the Christ* (meaning the *Anointed One)*, as spoken to his disciples; the central figure of Christianity and revered by Christians as the incarnation of God (second person of the Trinity) and as the Messiah; quote found in *The New Testament* (the Christian scriptures), taken from *The Gospel According to John,* chapter 8, verse 32.

22. Quote by Martin Luther King, Jr. (1929–1968), American Baptist minister and prominent civil rights leader, leader of the National Association of Colored People, received the 1964 Nobel Peace Prize; quote found on the website of *The King Center*, www.thekingcenter. org, home page.

23. Quote by Ervin Laszlo (1932–present), Hungarian philosopher of science, integral theorist and classical musician, contemporary leader in the field of science and philosophy; founder of the *Club of Budapest*; taken from *Science and the Akashic Field: An Integral Theory of Everything,* by Ervin Laszlo, Inner Traditions Publishing, 2007.

24. Quote by Plato (427–347 BCE), Classical Greek philosopher, mathematician and author; student of Socrates and teacher of Aristotle; founder of the Academy in Athens (the first institution of higher learning in the western world); quote found in one of Plato's dialogues exploring the nature of knowledge, *Theaetetus,* by Plato, Kessinger Publishing, 2004.

25. Quote by Epictetus (55–c. 135 AD), Greek Stoic philosopher; was born in Turkey, lived in Rome, and exiled to Greece; a strong influence on Roman emperor Marcus Aurelius; quote found in *The*

Discourses, by Arrian (Epictetus' most famous pupil), written c. 108 AD; quote taken from *Epictetus—The Discourses As Reported by Arrian, the Manual and Fragments,* by W. A. Oldfater, Grove Press, 2007.

26. Quote by Joseph Campbell; (1904–1987), American mythology professor, prolific writer and popular lecturer; considered an inspired authority on comparative mythology; quote found in *A Hero With a Thousand Faces,* originally published in 1949; New World Library (new edition), 2008.

27. Quote by St. Paul the Apostle (c. 5–67 AD), earlier known as Saul of Tarsus, called the Apostle to the Gentiles, notable early Christian missionary, and author of 14 Epistles in the *New Testament* (the Christian scriptures); quote found in the *New Testament,* and taken from the *Epistle to the Philippians,* chapter 4, verse 7.

28. Quote by Chuang-tzu (c. 369–c. 286 BCE), classical Chinese Taoist philosopher, often referred to in English as Master Chuang; famous for asserting that the world needs no government; quote found in *The Essential Tao: An Initiation into the Heart of Taoism Through the Authentic Tao Te Ching and the Inner Teachings of Chuang-Tzu,* translated by Thomas Cleary, HarperSanFrancisco, 1992.

29. Quote by Meister Eckhart (1260–1328), born Johann Eckhart von Hochheim, German Christian Dominican philosopher, theologian (teaching in Paris and Cologne) and mystic (some of whose mystical teachings were condemned by the Church); source of quote unknown.

30. Quote by Maharishi Mahesh Yogi (1917–2008), devoted disciple of Swami Brahmananda Saraswati, then a famous Indian Hindu guru, founder and teacher of the Transcendental Meditation technique and the TM Sidhi program, known for his efforts to create world peace; source of quote unknown.

31. Quote found in *Writing Our Story with Love,* author and source unknown.

32. Quote by Gabrielle Roth, modern musician, dancer, author and philosopher; known as "the urban shaman," she directs the theatre company *The Mirrors* and is the founder of *The Moving Center;*

quote found in *The Wisdom of Women,* edited by Carol Spenard Larusso, New World Library, 1992.

33. Quote by Ludwig Wittgenstein (1889–1951), Austrian-British philosopher, proponent of analytic and linguistic philosophy, generally recognized as one of the most influential philosophers of the 20th century; quote found in *Philosophical Investigations,* by Ludwig Wittgenstein, translated by G. E. M. Anscombe, Blackwell Publishers, 1969.

34. Quote by Henry David Thoreau (1817–1862), American naturalist, writer, transcendentalist, tax-resister and philosopher, best known for his book *Walden;* quote taken from *The Maine Woods: The Writings of Henry David Thoreau, vol. III,* by Henry David Thoreau, AMS Press, 1982.

35. Quote by Sam Walter Foss (1858–1911), American librarian and poet; his five volumes of poetry reflect themes of the common man; most known for his *The House By the Side of the Road;* quote found in *Simple Abundance: A Daybook of Comfort and Joy,* by Sarah Ban Breathnach, Grand Central Publishing, 1995.

36. Quote by Plato (427–347 BCE), Classical Greek philosopher, mathematician and author; student of Socrates and teacher of Aristotle; founder of the Academy in Athens (the first institution of higher learning in the western world); the words of the quote are those of Timaeus of Locri, as expressed in the theoretical treatise, *Timaeus,* by Plato, written in 360 BCE; quote is taken from *Timaeus,* by Plato, Dutton Adult Publishing, 1965.

37. Quote by Meister Eckhart (1260–1328), born Johann Eckhart von Hochheim, German Christian philosopher, theologian and mystic; quote found in *Da Vinci Decoded: Discovering the Spiritual Secrets of Leonardo's Seven Principles,* by Michael J. Gelb, Dell Publishing, 2004, p. 77.

38. Quote by Brian Swimme (1950–present), researcher, author and speaker in cosmology, evolution and religion; founder of the *Epic of Evolution Society*; quote taken from *The Hidden Heart of the Cosmos: Humanity and the New Story,* by Brian Swimme, Orbis Books, New York, 1996.

39. Quote by Joseph Campbell; (1904–1987), American mythology professor, prolific writer and popular lecturer; considered an inspired authority on comparative mythology; quote found in *The Power of Myth,* by Joseph Campbell, with Bill Moyers, Anchor Press, 1991.

40. Quote by St. Paul the Apostle (c. 5–67 AD), earlier known as Saul of Tarsus, called the Apostle to the Gentiles, notable early Christian missionary, and author of 14 Epistles in the *New Testament;* quote found in *The New Testament* (the Christian scriptures), taken from the *1ˢᵗ Epistle to the Corinthians,* written by St. Paul, chapter 3, verse 16.

41. Quote by Gautama Siddhartha (563–483 BCE), known as *the Buddha* ("the enlightened one"), famous Indian teacher, founder of Buddhism, generally recognized by Buddhists as the supreme Buddha of our age; source of quote unknown.

42. Quote by Eckhart Tolle (1948–present), Canadian (born in Germany) spiritual teacher, motivational speaker and writer on the mystical life; *The Power of Now: A Guide to Spiritual Enlightenment,* by Eckhart Tolle, New World Library, California, 1999.

43. Quote by Don Miguel Ruiz (1952–present), Mexican author, nagual, shaman and teacher; former medical doctor and surgeon; most known for his best-selling book *The Four Agreements;* quote taken from *Toltec Prophesies of Don Miguel Ruiz,* by Mary Carroll Nelson, Council Oaks Books, 2003.

44. Quote by Fred Alan Wolf (1934–present), theoretical physicist and popular writer on subjects of quantum physics and consciousness, a science popularizer on several television channels; quote taken from *Dr. Quantum's Little Book of Big Ideas: Where Science Meets Spirit,* Moment Point Press, by Fred Alan Wolf, 2005, p. 143.

45. Quote by Gabrielle Roth, modern musician, dancer, author and philosopher; known as "the urban shaman," she directs the theatre company *The Mirrors* and is the founder of *The Moving Center;* quote found on her website, www.gabrielleroth.com.

46. Quote found in *The Holographic Paradigm,* article found on the website www.thelovinggod.com; the holographic paradigm, first proposed by physicists David Bohm and Karl Pribram, posits

Your life is a sacred journey. And it is about change, growth, discovery, movement, transformation, continuously expanding your vision of what is possible, stretching your soul, learning to see clearly and deeply, listening to your intuition, taking courageous challenges at every step along the way.

You are on the path ... exactly where you are meant to be right now. ... And from here, you can only go forward, shaping your life story into a magnificent tale of triumph, of healing, of courage, of beauty, of wisdom, of power, of dignity and of love.

CAROLINE ADAMS[1]

that theories utilizing holographic structures can lead to a unified understanding of consciousness and life; the website cites the author of the article as unknown; however, reference can be made to *The Holographic Paradigm*, by Ken Wilber, Shambhala Press, 1982.

47. Quote by Novalis (1772–1801), born Georg Philipp Friedrich Freiherr von Heidenberg, author and philosopher of German Romanticism, known for his attempt to connect science, philosophy and poetry; quote found in *Pollen and Fragments: Selected Poetry and Prose of Novalis* (German title: *Blüthenstaub-Fragmente)*, by Novalis, Phanes Publishing, 1989.

48. Quote by Diane Arbus (1923–1971), American photographer, noted for her portraits of people living on the fringe of society; quote taken from the book, *Walking in this world: The Practical Art of Creativity*, by Julia Cameron, Penguin Books, 2003.

49. Quote by Albert Einstein (1879–1955), German-born theoretical physicist, best known for his theory of relativity, and winner of the 1921 Nobel Prize in Physics; named Person of the Century by *Time* magazine in 1999; quote found in *A Brief Biography of Albert Einstein*, by Rick Archer, April 2005, found on the website of the SSQQ Archives, www.ssqq.com/archive/alberteinstein.htm.

50. Quote by Stanley Lau, reportedly taken from *Confirmation*; neither author nor source could be found.

51. Quote by Hafiz (1329–1389), Persian (Iranian) Muslim poet and mystic, born Shams-ud-din-Muhammad; his poetry blends themes of love, mysticism and Sufism; quote taken from *Only One Rule*, poem by Hafiz, found in *The Gift: Poems by Hafiz, the Great Sufi Master*, Translations by Daniel Ladinsky, Penguin Books, 1999, p. 331.

BIBLIOGRAPHICAL REFERENCES

1. Quote by Caroline Adams (1961-present), American performance coach, motivational speaker and inspirational writer; quote found in *Bright Words for Dark Days: Meditations for Women Who Get the Blues*, by Caroline Adams Miller, Bantam Books, 1994.

ABOUT THE AUTHOR

Bill Bauman is one of the simplest people you'll ever meet—he just "is." Yet, his core essence calls him daily into selfless, expansive service to a human family he loves deeply. He feels called to be the voice of the purest truth possible—a truth without beliefs, complexities or codes of conduct ... that speaks purely to each person's soul ... that carries genuine unconditional love and respect. In this sacred space of being and allowing, Bill believes that each person is free to discover his or her own truth, love and empowerment—from within.

Bill is a unique blend of many perspectives. Through his life, he has lived sequentially and powerfully in the diverse worlds of philosophy, religion, psychology, business, politics and spirituality. Religiously, he has been a Catholic priest and Religious Science minister. As a licensed psychologist, he has specialized in deep psychotherapy and consulted in diverse settings. As a businessman, he has owned and operated three businesses and two non-profit organizations: World Peace Institute in Washington, DC and, currently, The Center for Soulful Living. Spiritually, he's been a gifted healer, blessed visionary and inspirational leader.

In the process, these many worlds and worldviews have found a unified home in Bill's consciousness. He is one with them all—and one with all people and approaches. Peacefully and quietly, he embraces everything, and enjoys a daily unity with life itself.

For three decades, Bill has known that part of his mission is to share his expanded vision with the world. This book is a strong piece of that calling. He thanks you for participating in the realization of that sacred charge by reading this book.

ALSO BY BILL BAUMAN

OZ POWER: How to Click Your Heels and Take Total Charge of Your Life

- *OZ POWER* Paperback book (210 pages)

- *OZ POWER* Audio book read by author (8 CDs, 9 hours)

- *The OZ POWER Companion: Inspirational Thoughts for Your Life's Journey*
  Spiral-bound, small-format book, 170 inspirational thoughts and affirmations
  from the *OZ POWER* paperback

- *OZ POWER A Presentation by Bill Bauman*
  Presentation of the spirit and content of *OZ POWER!*
  (video DVD or audio CD format, 37 minutes)

SOUL TALK

Presentation about the soul's four gifts: truth, power, love and empowerment
(video DVD or audio CD format, 25 minutes)

LIVING WITH GRACE

Presentation about the loving qualities of grace, and an invitation into grace's blessings
(video DVD or audio CD format, 25 minutes)

FINDING YOUR INNER TRUTH

Guided journey into your depths to discover your innate love, wisdom and truth
(video DVD or audio CD format, 25 minutes)

LIFE'S THREE ESSENTIAL TOOLS

Invitation into life's three magical tools: power, love and consciousness
(video DVD or audio CD format, 25 minutes)

INNER JOURNEYS ... OUTER MASTERY

Each volume contains four inspiring talks and meditations on four audio CDs

- Volume I: *The Real You ... Finding Purpose in Life ...*
  How Vast is Your Vision ... Living in the Moment

- Volume II: *The Spirit of Forgiveness ... Welcoming Life's Gifts ...*
  The Many-Faceted You ... Living with the Coyote

- Volume III: *Finding Your Inner Beauty ... Me, a Mystic? ...*
  Life!—the Soul's View ... A View from Above the Forest

**All products can be ordered from the Center for Soulful Living
website at www.aboutcsl.com.**

Breinigsville, PA USA
10 September 2009
223830BV00003BA/1/P